365 ways to Raise Confident kids*

365 ways to Raise Confident kids

Activities That Build Self-Esteem, Develop Character and Encourage Imagination

Sheila Ellison & Barbara Ann Barnett

SOURCEBOOKS, INC.®
NAPERVILLE, ILLINOIS

Published by Sourcebooks, Inc.
P.O. Box 372, Naperville, Illinois, 60566
(630) 961-3900
FAX: (630) 961-2168
www.sourcebooks.com

The Library of Congress has cataloged the previous edition as follows:

Ellison, Sheila.
        365 ways to raise great kids / Sheila Ellison and Barbara Ann Barnett.
                p. cm.
        ISBN 1-57071-398-7 (alk. paper)
        1. Parent and child—Miscellanea. 2. Child rearing—Miscellanea. 3. Creative activities
and seat work.
        4. Family recreation. I. Barnett, Barbara Ann. II. Title.
        HQ755.85.E46 1998
        649.'1—dc21   98-216
                CIP

Printed and bound in the United States of America.
                LB 10 9 8 7 6 5 4 3 2 1

Dedication

To all the caretakers of the world's children
in the hope that we can raise children who know who they are,
can say what they feel, and believe in all they can become.
And, to the many sources of inspiration to us in writing this book.

Sheila and Barbara Ann

Acknowledgments

I am especially grateful to my parents Nancy and Dave Maley for raising me with the belief that all people are valuable human beings, for believing in and teaching me the importance of caring for others, and for loving and encouraging me to believe in myself.

A heartfelt thanks to my publisher Dominique Raccah for her direction, insight, and belief in this book. To Todd Stocke, Renee Calomino, and Karen Bouris at Sourcebooks for their encouragement and hard work.

To the fifth graders in Tom Draggett's class at Ormondale School in Portola Valley, California, for their creative and wonderful illustrations.

Sheila

Contents

Introduction

Parents spend their lives growing their children, guiding decisions, giving ideas, working through problems and modeling behaviors, hoping that someday their child will have gained the skills necessary to shine brightly out in the world on their own. We walk hand in hand down life's path teaching what we know, passing on what we believe, and communicating life's challenges until our children are ready to walk alone. Our love guides and encourages our children to find their most creative spirit, a spirit that believes it can soar.

Everything you do, everything you think, everything you believe and every action you take has an effect on how your child grows. It is not possible for a child to be better than the example you are setting. So as parents we have the most wonderful job on earth, that of shaping another human being simply by living each day. It is not about doing everything right, or knowing every listening skill, or using the correct form of discipline, or having all the knowledge—it is about wanting to. Just having the desire and making the effort to do the best you can is enough for your child to grow. Your child will feel your attitude. They will know that the person they become matters to you.

365 Ways to Raise Confident Kids is designed to help you find everyday ways to share what you believe, what you value, and what you think is important for your children to learn. This book will give you the tools you need to accomplish what all parents want: to raise bright, caring, honest, happy, respectful and creative children. The 365 activities will put in your hands a concrete, day-to-day guide for building character and teaching values and life skills which will improve life for everyone in the family. Each activity experienced becomes a seed planted in your child's mind that will blossom into a field of behaviors, strengthening your child for life.

The activities contained in this book can each be done individually. There is no need to do them in order, nor is it necessary to do one before understanding another. They are simple in form so they can be easily understood and put into action. You know your family and its needs better than anyone else. The best place to start is in an area of personal interest, or where you feel your family would most benefit. If you are unsure where to start, start at the beginning. As you experience the activities, you may come up with new ideas. Allow yourselves the freedom to expand and grow in your own direction.

The book is divided into seven parts. **Part One: About Yourself,** addresses the necessity of having a positive relationship with your self, which is essential in order to achieve happiness. It includes the concepts of self-esteem, self-motivation, resourcefulness, spending time alone, and developing imagination.

Part Two: Express Yourself, teaches ways to confidently and courageously express feelings, while at the same time working on the interpersonal communication skills needed to communicate effectively with others. The importance of positive, appreciative and affectionate touching as a means of non-verbal communication is also discussed.

Part Three: About Others, introduces ways to strengthen relationships with others as we begin to understand how to nurture those connections. The topics covered are caring for others, developing friendships, learning to respect others, cooperation, being open to change in our lives, having good manners, and reaching out into the community in a caring way.

Part Four: Building Character, is about developing specific character traits like courage, honesty, patience, tolerance, helpfulness, responsibility, discipline, and forgiveness. These are the personal building blocks that create human beings who have the innate ability to make positive contributions to our world.

Part Five: Challenges, helps us understand and accept the challenges and difficulties we all experience throughout life. Exposing children to activities on death and troubled times prepares them to remain unafraid, open, balanced, and close to the family when the hard times hit.

Part Six: Family Matters, is about family life. The activities will give each person the sense they are an important member of their family—a family that has a life, a history, shared experiences, meaningful connections, and a long, long future. Topics covered include family history, mom's time, dad's time, how parents relate to each other, sibling relationships, how older people relate to younger people, and how to have a family meeting.

Part Seven: Having Fun Together, reveals the secret to family members staying close to each other in their hearts—having fun together! If we can have fun and play games together, if we can laugh and develop a sense of humor, if we can build traditions that everyone enjoys, then we will have added the spice that makes all the effort worthwhile.

The activities are simply experiences you will share. Doing any ten activities from the book will positively change your family. Your children will see and experience you being a living example. As parents, you can tell your children how you think, you can moralize, and you can explain what you expect. But it is only when you demonstrate what you mean by how you live your life that you become an effective teacher. When they witness in your actions what you have been saying with your words, it changes them. The activities contained in this book will give you what you need to be an effective teacher.

The day a child enters our lives, our feet are placed upon the path that leads us on an enormous journey—one where there is no stopping, no turning back, and no bailing out. This journey lasts a lifetime. Every day we take a step forward in some direction. With each new adventure we learn new skills. When people begin a journey they do some planning. They usually have some sort of guidebook that tells them where to go, what to look for, and how to get where they want to be. This book is intended to be used as a guidebook for parents who have courageously taken on the responsibility of shaping a child's life. Along the journey, when you least expect it, you will have moments when your heart beats with joy as you realize your child "got it." You will feel invincible in these moments, like all your dedication, love, and understanding meant something immeasurably valuable. And you'll be right.

Part One:
About Yourself

Self-Esteem

A child's self-esteem begins to be formed very early, and continues being created day by day. Self-esteem comes from learning to accept who we are by seeing the insufficiencies and still choosing to like ourselves. Every child's self-esteem grows with each experience of successful interaction, a job well done, a goal met, as well as through the positive words of the ones we love. Self-esteem doesn't depend on huge accomplishments. It depends on the small daily tasks that build a child's belief that they can handle their life and handle it well.

"We are the hero of our own story."
—Mary McCarthy

Feel Good Notebook

Buy each member of the family a small spiral-bound notebook or journal to write in. Each night after dinner or before bed, have everybody write six things in their journal that made them feel good that day. The idea is to focus on the positive experiences we all have. So often the bad or worrisome experience is remembered and the simple smile, the fun game at recess, the baby bird seen, or the laughter at a good joke, goes unnoticed. Feel free to share what has been written, or keep it private. If a child is too young to write, he could draw pictures or dictate to someone else. If nothing comes to mind, help him by bringing up the day's events: games played at pre-school, friends they walked home from school with, or a dinner they liked. Make your family one that spends each day searching for, and finding the positive.

Outline the Good Qualities

Self-esteem is something that grows throughout a person's life. It is a belief in one's self, an ability to see the good qualities within, as well as a growing confidence in one's choices. Since children are so dependent on the attitude and opinion of their parents and siblings, the family is the first place where self-esteem starts to grow. Take the time to talk about each person's good qualities in a fun way. Draw an outline of each person's hand on separate pieces of paper. Take one hand at a time and talk about the person whose hand is drawn. What do they do well? What do you like about them? How do they contribute to the family? What kind of qualities do they have? Write all these things inside and around the outlined hands. Do this with each family member, and when finished hang up each outline for everyone to see. If you think of additional qualities over time, feel free to add them to your drawings.

I Like Me Poster

Sometimes we focus so hard on the things we need to do, the new skills we are trying to learn, and the things that need improvement, that we lose sight of the great person we already are! Take the time to look at, and appreciate all the things you like to do, the friends you have, the person you have grown to be. Have everyone get a piece of poster board, scissors, glue stick, photographs, and old magazines. The idea is to make a poster that is all about you. Include anything you like. Feel free to write words, glue on pictures of friends, family, your hobbies and interests, or even a homework paper you were proud of. Each person can hang their poster up with pride! This project is for everyone to do together—it isn't just for the kids. Parents need to celebrate their good qualities too!

Circle Dance

Here's a way to start the day that will put everyone in a good mood! Get the family in a circle and hold hands. Start walking, running, hopping, or tiptoeing around in a circle and chant one of the following sentences at a time. The sentences should be things about your family that you all believe: we are loving, we are kind, we are smart, we have fun, we get along, we like to help, we are a team. The oldest person starts by saying one of these sentences, then everyone says it a few times together. Anyone can change the chant when they want, just make sure everyone says each chosen chant at least three times. Older kids (8 and up) may think this is stupid but younger kids think it's fun; they especially like to see their parents smiling and moving in a circle with them.

Giving Specific Complaints

So often when we tell someone they did something well we say it in general terms: you did a good job, you are a good mom, thanks for cleaning up, you are a good student. Play "Get Specific" some night after dinner. Each person will get a chance to be complimented by the family. Start by stating something very general and then become more and more specific. Here's are some examples: you are a great dad; you cook great dinners; you make a great Mexican dinner; you cook the tortillas just right; you make all the right ingredients; you serve the best guacamole, etc. Here's another example: you did a good job this morning; you made your bed without being asked; you got all the sheets folded under the mattress; you smoothed out the cover nicely; your stuffed animals were arranged so cute. Kids especially need to hear exactly what you liked about what they did, so they can repeat it!

5

Planting Positive Seeds of Thought

If you want tomatoes, you don't plant carrot seeds. If you want high self-esteem you don't plant seeds of negative thought. The seeds we plant in our minds are the thoughts we have, the positive or negative "self-talk" we use. How often do we use words that bring us down or hold us back: "I am really terrible at math," "So-and-so hates me," "I can't do anything right." All of these thoughts are seeds that can grow into who you will be tomorrow. Help your children practice self-talk. Take small pieces of paper and write one seed of positive self-talk on each paper. Have each person do at least five. Now everyone fold up these pieces of paper and take them outside to some dirt, dig a hole, and bury them. Plant something beautiful, or sprinkle some seeds that will grow over the planted paper as a reminder for your family to plant the thoughts in their minds that they most want to grow.

Each Person Takes Center Stage

Simply paying attention to someone can raise their self-esteem. Give each person in the family five to ten minutes to take center stage. They can do or say anything they would like: sing a song, tell a story, read a poem, explain the game of baseball, do a trick, tell a joke or talk about their day. The audience is not critical in any way; just listen, watch, laugh, and clap. It feels good to fully express yourself, and have the whole family support your expression.

Get Homework Done

Children spend much of their time at school. Understanding assignments and getting them done on time makes a child feel proud, and in control of his life. Help your child organize his "work" in a way that makes it easy for him to remember assignments, work peacefully, and be able to get help if needed. Sit down and tell your child how important you think homework is and that you are willing to help. Together, brainstorm ideas to make homework an easy task for both of you. Here are some ideas:

- Get a small notebook in which to write every homework assignment. Make sure the parent glances in this each day. Buy a binder that can be divided into different subjects.

- Talk about taking one minute to think after school before running out of the classroom for home to make sure all the needed books and worksheets are in the backpack.

- Set up a space at home where the child will not be distracted. Stock it with paper, pencils, dictionary, eraser, ruler.

- In the beginning set a timer for 25 minute intervals, taking at least a five minute break after each work time. Parents should supervise study time.

- Parent should be available to answer questions or look over work. Parent should not do the homework for the child. Working through the problems and finishing it themselves will build the child's sense of self. If a parent does the homework, the child thinks they are not capable.

If at any time you feel your child is having trouble, meet with his teacher.

We're a Great Family Because...

Families are great in many different ways. Sit in a circle and have each member finish the sentence: "We are a great family because..." Go around the circle many times with all the positive things you can think of: things you like to do together, how the house is kept, shared goals. Just living in a family takes work, love, and courage, so it's important to keep in mind just how special all of you are.

6

My Personal Scrapbook

Remember the feeling you get when you look back on a past event and the memories fill your mind? That feeling of "Wow, I really did that?" or "That was so much fun, I wish we still lived there." Memories of past experiences give children a sense of personal history and self-understanding. Looking back will help them to realize that their past experiences affect who they are today. Get a big blank book to start a scrapbook. Encourage your child to save things like ticket stubs, special cards, artwork, special homework reports, pictures from special events, and postcards. Make sure that when something is put in the scrapbook, a little is written about the event: who went with them, what they liked about it and the date they went. It might be fun to pick one day per month to update everyone's scrapbooks together.

Give a Morning Boost

Before you go to bed tonight, think about something another family member did today that you liked. Write a note or draw a picture about it to be given to the person at breakfast. You might even put the note on the table where they sit each morning to surprise them. This is a great way to help someone else start their day in a good way. It's also a great surprise to put a note in someone's lunch.

Emphasizing "Pull-Ups"

Put-downs are negative comments made towards another person that lower self-esteem. Get your family together and talk about put-downs and pull-ups. Give everyone three minutes to think of all the put-downs they hear: "you're stupid," "you can't do anything right," "you're a pig," "nobody likes you." Then take three minutes and think of all the pull-ups: "good job," "what a good decision," "I'm so proud of you." What was easier to think of? What is more fun to hear? What makes you feel better? Talk about having an agreed upon signal if someone hears a put-down: a hand held up indicating "halt," a hiss, two fingers raised in the peace sign. Kids will love hissing and halting, and as always, humor has a way of pointing out and changing behavior better than yelling ever could.

Like Yourself!

It's not enough for other people to appreciate and like things about you, you have to like yourself too. Sit down with your child and make a list of all the things your child likes about herself. If your child is old enough, you might want to create a form and have each person in the family fill one in. Label the categories as follows: looks, abilities or talents, friendships, habits, and feelings. Under each category have your child list at least five things he likes about himself. If he is having a hard time coming up with something, ask him questions such as, "What do you like most about your face?" "What are some of the things you do well?" or "Why do you think your friends like you?"

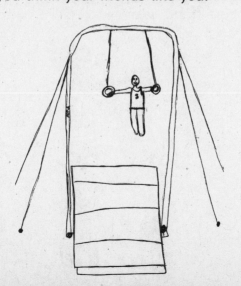

Supporting Each Other's Self-Expression

You'll need a tape recorder and enough blank tapes for each member of the family. The idea is for each person to record themselves doing, saying, singing, or reciting whatever they want. They can make the tape alone or invite other family members to be part of their tape. Give everyone a few weeks to make their tapes. The tapes don't have to be any specific length, and adults should participate as well. Plan a listening party with refreshments. As each tape is played, support each other's self-expression. No negative comments allowed! Having a happy adulthood is, in part, about finding and expressing your own voice. Give your child an encouraging start.

Singing Your Own Song

Kids love to make up new words to songs they already know. They especially like to hear adults singing silly words to songs they recognize. Take a song everyone knows: "Twinkle, Twinkle Little Star," "Row Row Row Your Boat." The theme of the song will be "I like myself today." Take this phrase and have everyone participate in making up new words. When the song is complete, write down the words and sing it at least once! Silliness can be its own reward.

Oh, Liz is in show biz!

Confidence in Conversation

Learning something new, then being able to use the new skill, makes children very proud of themselves. An active and growing vocabulary is a fun new skill that the family can work on together. Pick one word a week and post it on the refrigerator. Say the word a few times so your child knows how to pronounce it. Tell them the definition and how to use it in a sentence or two. The challenge is for everyone to use that word at least once each day in their conversations at school, work, or home. Tell everyone how you used the word then give yourself a point. The more you use the word, the more points you earn. At the end of the month, whoever has the most points is declared "Grand Vocabulary Champion"!

Nature Names

Native Americans give nature names to the people in their tribe. They are words from nature that describe the person's strongest characteristics or an life experience the person had with the nature entity; such as Sunbeam, Little River, Rugged Mountain, Night Sky, Dolphin, Water Lily, Drifting Cloud, Turtle, Hawk, Meadowlark, Singing Wolf, Honeybee, or Sunflower. Is there something in nature that reminds you of yourself? Get together as a group and think of all the nature names that describe each of you. Make sure this is a sharing of good qualities you see in nature (Mud Puddle, because you are so dirty, or Rooster, because you crow so loud in the morning, are not names that will build self-esteem!). If you find a name you like, let that be your nature nickname.

Welcome Home

Kings and queens announced their arrival with trumpets blasting. Why not have instruments available for individuals to announce their arrival at your front door: a set of bells, wind chimes, or a xylophone would work well. Each person could make up their own melody that would be recognized upon entering. Every time a family member comes home from school, work, or activity, they play their song. Traditions like this create lasting memories for children of family life and rituals.

Self-Motivation

Self-motivation is the impulse to soar. It is the little kernel of hope inside each one of us that allows us to set goals—that moves us to reach higher. It is the reason a person goes on, even when they want to quit. It is the belief that something can be done, even when the odds are against it. When a person is motivated, nobody can take away their power to move forward, and when that motivation comes from inside a person's heart they become unbeatable.

"One can never consent to creep when one feels an impulse to soar."
—Helen Keller

Dream File

Dreaming about things you may want in your life is one of the great motivators. Encourage your children to dream by sharing their dreams with each other. Start a dream file that will contain pictures or descriptions of the family's material dreams. Use articles, newspapers, or magazines to find and cut out pictures of homes, vacation spots, cars, bikes, instruments or whatever inspires. Put everything you cut out into a special file. You may even want to glue the pictures onto a piece of paper, write your name, and date it. Keep this file in a special place and encourage everyone to add to it now and then. Have fun and give your imagination free reign. Make sure each person understands how important, special, and private each family member's dreams are. You might be amazed by the dreams that actually come true.

Goal Cards

Everyone in the family gets one 5" x 8" index card. On one side, write a single goal; on the other side, write the steps you will take to accomplish that goal. Think through, or talk about, the steps needed to reach the particular goal. At the end of the day, or once a week, briefly write on the front of the card, underneath your written goal, what you did towards accomplishing the goal. Date each entry so you can each see how you continued to work toward the desired end. You may want to do more than one goal card at a time, especially since there are some goals that can be accomplished in a week, while others may take years. This will help children develop the habit of thinking about the direction they need to go in order to accomplish something. It also shows them that action taken toward a goal actually helps them reach it.

Self-Talk Strategies

Often times, our own internal voice sounds the loudest when pointing out faults. It may be a quiet voice that says things like: "I can't write that paper," "Everyone in the class will beat me if I race," "The dinner tasted terrible, I'm an awful cook," or "The house never looks clean enough." It's a known fact that bad thoughts make a person feel worse, and do worse. Positive thoughts, on the other hand, make a person feel better and do better. The more positive self-talk a child can repeat to themselves, the better they will feel, and the better they will do. Sit down with your child and make a long list of positive thoughts they have about their own abilities. If they don't have many, suggest making some up based on ways they would like to feel in a given situation. Make a deal with your child: the next time they hear a voice in their head saying negative things, they have to come to you with the list the two of you made up. Together, pick a positive thought off the list and repeat it out loud five times; then, encourage your child to keep repeating it throughout the day whenever negative things pop into their head.

I Think I Can, I Think I Can

Remember that lovely children's story about the train who couldn't make it up the hill, so he started chanting, "I think I can, I think I can"? If you have never read the story, go to the library and check it out; it's called *The Little Engine That Could*. The next time you hear someone in your family saying "I can't do it," get the family together and tell them the story. Talk about how attitude makes all the difference. From now on, whenever a family member says "I can't do it," or is afraid to try something new, anyone else in the family can simply say "I think I can" to remind the person of the story. One of the beauties of being part of a family is that you have shared memories. So, when a family member is about to jump into a pool to swim a scary race that they don't think they can win, it only takes a few words to inspire them. You don't have to sit down and talk about how much you believe in them, how they should think positive and do the best they can; you can simply look them in the eye, smile, and say, "I think I can."

Do You Have a Hero?

Every child needs someone they can look up to, someone who has qualities the child can model, someone who has accomplished something the child wants. Sometimes the parent is a child's hero, sometimes a sports star, a teacher, writer, musician, or actor. The important thing is that whenever great qualities in people are pointed out to your child, they will learn something about what a hero is. Ask your child if they can name two people whom they admire and want to be like. Talk about the reasons they like these people. Is there anything your child can do to be like these heroes? Admiration is a great self-motivator, so encourage your child's belief in everyday heroes as well as history's great heroes.

Start a Business

There are many businesses that kids can start and run with little or no money. If your child has time on her hands and wants to give business a try, some ideas that work include: designing stationery, taking care of children or pets, having a lemonade stand, tutoring math or reading for younger children, helping an elderly neighbor do their shopping or yard work, washing cars or pets, walking a dog, weeding or raking up leaves. The options are endless. In fact, you'll find a number of books on the subject at your local library. But first talk to your child about what the responsibility of being a good worker involves, including being on time, doing what you say you will, and listening to instructions. Help your child get started by teaching him any skill he may lack, and helping him decide what he will charge for his service. Design a flyer and give it out to neighbors and friends. Being in charge, making a little money, and feeling good about a job well done are all self-motivators.

I Want to Quit

When a child decides to enroll in an activity like soccer, basketball, dance, piano lessons, art class, the two of you should make a commitment to try the activity for a period of time. With a sport, they may have to agree to stick with it for the ten week season. And certainly with any musical instrument, make sure your child gives it a good several months. Many times a child will lack confidence in the beginning. They see other children who might be better than they are, or decide they don't like practicing and want to quit. Finishing something they start is a good habit that shows the child they can overcome their fears and learn new skills. This success will help them to be self-motivated in the future, as they have experienced their own strengths and weaknesses, and worked through them. If your child participates for the agreed time, and then wants to quit, respect her decision. If your child is not interested in an outside activity, look for one together and encourage their involvement.

Mapping Out Plans

Kids don't usually become totally self-directed until sometime in late adolescence. Until that time, they need help and guidance from the adults around them. They need to be taught strategies of planning, and they need to see how their parents set goals and accomplish them. Buy your children a big calendar and encourage them to write the following things: dates school reports are due, special events having to do with school, their athletic teams, recitals, school holidays. When your children come home with large projects from school, ask questions about it so they can start to organize how they might approach it. For example, writing a report: "What kind of report does it need to be? What if that book isn't at the library? What if you have to go away next weekend?" Write on the calendar what needs to be done on the report, and by what date. Helping a child learn to break up large tasks into smaller goals gives them a tool to use for the rest of their life.

Looking Good, Feeling Neat

Teaching a child good grooming habits isn't always easy. Sometimes it takes reminder after reminder. On an occasion when your children look extra clean and neat, take a picture of them. Another time when your child looks extra sloppy, take a picture. Expressing a sense of humor, mount both pictures on the same board next to each other. Do the same with your child's room, taking one picture clean and one picture messy. Then talk to your child about the things they would need to do in order to look and feel neat all the time. Together make up a checklist for them to check off their neatness accomplishments each day, which would include each step they might take to look or feel neat: brush teeth, wash face, brush hair, put on deodorant make bed, fold clothes. Tell them how important it is to have good grooming habits, not just for cleanliness, but for the people who have to live with them.

Resourcefulness

Life for a child is all about learning how to weather the little storms each day brings. Being resourceful means taking on challenges, taking the time to think through those challenges, and then using available resources to solve them. Developing resourcefulness gives a child life skills for weathering their storms. It provides confidence to create options, and it shows them how to be proactive participants in the world around them.

"I am not afraid of storms, for I am learning how to sail my ship."
—Louisa May Alcott

Teach Everyday Skills

Everyday household skills like doing laundry, shopping, paying bills, and cleaning are important for a child to learn. They teach a child to be independent. When a child leaves your home with these skills, he will feel more self-confidence and you will worry less.

- Next time you go to the grocery store, take your child with you. Walk around the store together, showing him where to find the price, how to pick good fruit, where to find the ingredient labels. On the next trip give him a pile of coupons and tell him to find each item that is on the coupon and bring it back to your cart.

- If you have old checks, have your child practice filling them out. Show him what a bill looks like and how to address an envelope to send it. To balance a checkbook, simple addition and subtraction skills are required—why not assign your eight-year-old this task? (Of course, you will want to double check it.)

- Get the kids involved in sorting the laundry into light, dark, and white piles. Show them how to work the washer and dryer and encourage them to do their own laundry.

- Cooking skills need to be taught. Have a different child as kitchen helper each day.

Make a Room Border

Children enjoy decorating their rooms with things they make. Why not make a border around the top of the wall with homemade 8" x 10" artwork? They will get the satisfaction of using something they created for a "grown-up" purpose. It could be a painting, pencil drawing, poem, letter received, or award. Save pictures until you have enough to go around the top of the wall. Paste the pictures up with wallpaper paste, then once dry, go over the top of them with a clear acrylic (found at an artist supply shop). These pictures can be layered on top of each other just like wallpaper. So, if your child gets sick of the border, cover it up with new pictures.

Somewhere There's a Book

Children are curious creatures. Take a minute to reflect on what you usually do when your children ask questions. One kind of response that is time-consuming, but builds richness into relationships, is to get a book, read it together, and discover the answer that will satisfy the child's curiosity. When you do this you are teaching your child how to find the answer, where to look, how to use resources. They will learn that finding the answer to questions can be fun, and will quickly learn how to find the answers themselves.

Take Control

Many times children would like more control over something in their lives, such as how late they can stay up, what they can wear, when to do their homework or who they hang out with. Encourage discussion about control and listen to what your child has to say. Is there something in your child's life that they would like changed? If what your child has to say makes sense to you, work on a compromise that you both can live with. If what your child wants does not work for you, explain why.

Organize Yourself

Take the day to organize your desk, drawers, and closet, and have your children get involved by organizing their own things. You might want to color code your closet so everything of the same color is together, or you might want things together by type (slacks, blouses, dresses, shirts). While going through your clothes make sure to make a giveaway pile for clothes you don't wear enough to keep. Organization is a skill that children might need help with in the beginning, but after they are taught what to do, parents can step back and let them organize themselves. It helps to plan a monthly organization day where everyone in the family takes some time to organize themselves. On this day, make sure to spend the first part of the time with your child, teaching them how to get organized.

Setting Goals

The first twenty years of life are spent in a sort of training: learning the discipline it takes to live independently. You can't have self-discipline without training; you can't train without setting goals. Practice is the key, so put the whole family into training for something you can all do together, like a hike. The family will learn together that commitment, practice, acceptance of limitations, and encouragement all help in learning the self-discipline required to reach a goal. After you have completed training and have taken the hike together, be sure to celebrate. You might want to talk afterward about another goal to set and accomplish together.

Design Business Cards

Your child has as many friends as you do. He also meets new people all the time. Why not help him design his own name card so he can give it to his friends? If your child has certain skills he wants to offer like baby-sitting, yard work, pet care, car washing or dog walking, he can write that skill on the card also. Have him design the card by including his own artwork, picking the print style and color, and deciding just what he wants to say. He may simply want his name, address, and phone number. Make sure he understands that these cards are to be given only to people he knows, and want to be friends with.

Teach Yourself Something New

When was the last time you learned something new? Children who see their parents learning new skills will want to learn new skills themselves. Encourage your children's curiosity and guide them in finding the information they need to learn a skill. You may even want to find something new you can learn together. Some fun ideas might include learning to type, sign language, tap dance, calligraphy, sewing, astronomy, sports, yoga, a foreign language or playing a musical instrument. Children are incredibly resourceful with a little direction. Libraries are a great place to start since many skills can be taught simply by reading a book. Community recreation facilities often have classes open to all ages. Be encouraging and supportive of whatever new skills your child wants to pursue, at the same time allowing your child to do most of the work.

New Room Decorations

Next time your child says she is sick of her current bedroom, let her redesign it. Tell her to come up with a plan. Give her a budget to work from. Let her know the rules of what can and cannot be done: you will make her new curtains if she finds material, new furniture cannot be bought, they can paint a design on their wall. Once the child has come up with a plan you both agree to, let her get started. Teach her any skills you know that she may not, like how to use a paintbrush. The room may not turn out perfectly as if a professional designer did it, but your child will be thrilled with her creation. And, the experience of using her own resources will teach her more than having a perfect room.

If You Could Spend...

Pretend you have $10,000 (you can vary this amount depending on the age of the child). Give every member of your family a week to come up with the list of things they would buy. They have to find out approximate cost of the things they want to buy. Using a calculator they can compute how much their money will buy. They will decide what they simply must have, and what they will have to mark off their list. Give bonus praise for family members who decide to give some of their money to someone else who needs it. This exercise can help teach a child the monetary value of things, and the skills it takes to be a wise consumer.

Separate Time

Only when we are alone and silent do we hear our own voice. Children who value their own thoughts learn to understand their feelings. The child who is encouraged to entertain himself with a solitary interest learns to think independently. In a world where everything seems fast and furious, the child who is comfortable within himself will find peace, and enjoy his own mind.

"Being solitary is being alone well."
—Alice Koller

Introducing Alone Time

There is a big difference between feeling lonely and spending time alone. Children may not know how to spend time alone with themselves. They may need to be introduced to the concept. Adults, on the other hand, usually treasure their time alone. Sit down and tell your children what you do in your alone time, and why you like it so much. Tell them what you get out of it. After you tell them about your alone time, ask each one to think of something they would like to do in their alone time. Pick a time today for everyone to spend thirty minutes of quiet, alone time. Be available to the children for the first time to offer encouragement and ideas.

Sounds of Silence

There is so much commotion in the days of most families that it's hard to find the time to stop and listen in silence. Yet, when we sit quietly and listen to the sounds around us, the world seems to come alive. Take ten minutes to each sit alone quietly, closing your eyes, and doing nothing but listening. You can all go outside, or simply sit inside the house. Set a timer; when it rings, everyone come together and talk about what they heard, and how it felt to listen in silence.

Hobby Tales

Having a hobby is more important than you might think; it gives a feeling of accomplishment, it is relaxing, and can be done alone. Hobbies teach children how to entertain themselves, how to develop an interest in something, and how to share their interests with others. If your children don't have a solitary hobby like listening to music, collecting something, reading, drawing, poetry writing, flower arranging or photography, take the time to introduce the concept. A good way to begin is by telling them the story behind your own hobby. Tell them how you got started, who helped you, what you liked about it, how you feel when you're doing it, and what you've learned from it. Take time to discuss the areas of interest your children already have. Together, come up with a hobby they might like to start, and help them get started. Remember, your children model their behavior after you, so if you sit around all day and watch TV, so will they!

Being Uninterrupted

Have you ever relaxed in your home, knowing for sure you wouldn't be interrupted? It's guaranteed that you'll benefit as a family if you do. Set aside two hours in the evening. Unplug the phone, television, stereo, and computer. Then put a note on the door notifying visitors you are unavailable. Do it when no one has to be anywhere else. During this time, don't try to accomplish things: no work, no housework, no homework, no chores. Simply do things you enjoy, either alone or together. When you claim the right to uninterrupted time, you will all feel a sense of retreat from the world's busy-ness.

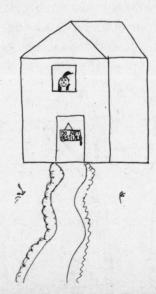

Thinking Time

Alone time is the very best time to discover all the things you can think about. Sometimes called "daydreaming," thinking of nothing in particular is not usually encouraged. Yet, it's so much fun. Everyone take ten minutes to go someplace alone and think. Think about the things that make you happy, people you like, places you want to go, summertime, or your next birthday party. After ten minutes, come back together and let the kids say whether they liked this or not. Encourage them to use this thinking time when they are feeling upset, sad, or bored.

Kids Have Time

Kids have the time it takes to develop their interests. But it also takes is a little encouragement from a parent. It's not a parent's job to entertain a child all the time. Somehow, children have to learn to motivate themselves and use the time they have alone in a positive way. Here's how to get them started. Pay attention to things such as any interests they seem to have, what they talk about, what questions they ask, what brings an animated look to their face. Open up an ongoing conversation to discover more and more what they might like to do. Listen well, then put out suggestions of interests that might suit them. Your job is to encourage, support, help with supplies, teach skills, supervise if asked, cheer them on, and make a big deal of their accomplishments.

Alone in the Wild

It's fun to explore nature together as a family. Pick a whole day or an afternoon to spend in your favorite wilderness area. For each child in the family, take along a large ball of twine. Once you are all at your chosen outdoor location, and have established your "home base," tie an end of twine around the wrist of each child who wants to go off on an adventure alone in the wild. Then, let them go off to explore on their own, feeling secure they'll find their way back by following their twine. If not all the children are old enough, or interested enough in exploring nature alone like this, they might create a piece of artwork by assembling things they find around the home base. If your child is old enough to find her way back to the home base without the twine, make sure she has a watch and a specific time at which to return.

Imagination

When a mind is allowed the freedom to fly high and wild with imaginative thought, the inner view changes and the world looks different. Let each child dream, placing no limits on their thoughts, writing, inventions, masterpieces, or concepts. When a child's imagination is encouraged, it continues to grow and produce creatively. Remember: what you can see, you can be.

"Imagination is the highest kite
one can fly."
—Lauren Bacall

Imagine Your Future

Being able to imagine what your future will look like is part of what dreaming is all about. Children don't always know what they want to happen in their future. Talking together about different options and letting them know that you believe anything is possible will help them to use their imagination when creating an image of the future. Each person gets their own piece of posterboard, glue, scissors, and some old magazines. Begin cutting out pictures of things you imagine will be in your life. Don't be realistic. Be a dreamer, letting your mind run free. Include words, hand-drawn images, photographs, or anything you want. Hang this on the wall where you see it often, and add to it whenever you find

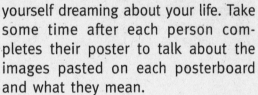

yourself dreaming about your life. Take some time after each person completes their poster to talk about the images pasted on each posterboard and what they mean.

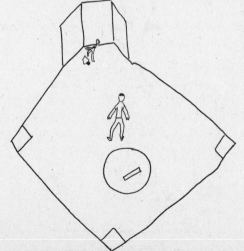

Change Channels

The next time your family watches TV together, notice how someone changes the channels whenever a show comes on they don't want to watch. Teach your children how to change channels in their mind when they are experiencing or thinking about something that causes them stress, worry, or fear. Here's how it works: whenever the unpleasant thought or experience happens, tell them to close their eyes and see in their mind something that will calm them down or make them feel better like playing with a friend, sitting in the forest or reading a good book. They might even want to develop different channels, like a good mood channel, a courage channel, or a patience channel, to which they can return whenever the need arises.

Great Thinkers

Some of the greatest thinkers and creators in history were renowned for imagining their creations first. Inspire your children with biographies on people like Leonardo da Vinci, Sir Isaac Newton, Wolfgang Mozart, and Albert Einstein. Talk about the value of imagination and problem solving as one of humanity's most important tools on the road to creating. Encourage this skill in your children. When they give you ideas that might sound silly or impractical, go with their train of thought instead of telling them something wouldn't work. Develop what they are saying by adding ideas of your own. This gives what they are imagining importance. It's the exercise in thinking that counts.

Cloud Stories

Nature has an imagination. It reshapes itself every moment in the movement of clouds. Have everyone get a blanket to lie on, and go outside together on a day when the sky is full of clouds. Start by looking at the shapes. Tell each other what the clouds look like to you. Use your imagination and tell stories about the shapes you see. You might see a cloud king, a magic white whale, or even a whipped cream pie that could heal the world. Listen to the stories, helping each other if the story line falters. Using your imagination is like taking a stroll in your mind. Free thinkers with big imaginations are the people who go on to invent computers, discover new medicine, write novels, etc. Encourage your child to keep imagining.

Imagine the Presents

Having a good imagination can teach children how to think their way out of almost anything: when you have no money, it helps you to think of ways to live. When a business is failing, the imaginative person searches for creative solutions. When a friend has done something that hurts, a thinking child comes up with solutions. Here's an example of a way to model such creativity. When you are short on money for a birthday or holiday season and presents are hard to come by, do the following: wrap up the presents you do have to make them look like many (divide the packages of underwear into three), then glue a picture of the present you really wanted to get them on the package. Tell them what you did and why you did it as they look at the taped on pictures. Chances are that the kids already knew you were having financial troubles, and they will think it's fun that you took their present request to heart even if it's simply a picture.

What It's Like to Work

Start to collect things you use at work, like cashed checks, old reports, calculator, phone, brief case and business cards. Take the time to explain to your child how each is used. Let your child use their imagination and pretend what it is like to have your job. Encourage them to ask you questions about anything they want to know about. If you have any adult friends who have jobs that interest your child, arrange an interview so your child can find out about their job. Knowing the kinds of jobs available, and what the people actually do each day on the job, will get your child thinking. It will give them ideas of jobs they might like. Who knows? That interview at eight might affect a career choice at twenty.

On the Answering Machine

It seems everyone has an answering machine these days. Get the family together and dream up a creative phone greeting. Each person can participate in the design, as well as the actual talking. It's fun to change the greeting each week: give a vacation report, a birthday announcement, a humorous reason you can't make it to the phone. Your friends will start calling just to see what "that creative family" came up with!

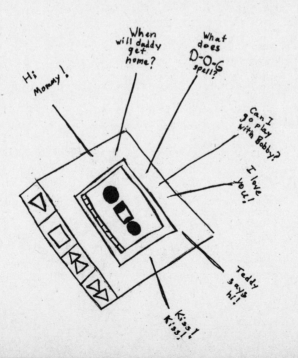

Part Two:
Express Yourself

Feelings

"Our feelings are our most genuine paths to knowledge."
—Audre Lorde

If you're brave enough to follow the path of a feeling to the end of the trail, you will gain knowledge straight from your own heart. Feelings are the guideposts that mark our way in life. They need to be felt, expressed, taken into consideration, and valued as the only true way to measure where we are. Feelings exist in all forms—from the wonderful feeling of love, to the difficult feeling of anger. Families who support the experiencing and interchange of feelings enjoy one of the deepest gifts of life.

"Those who do not know how to weep with their whole heart don't know how to laugh either."
—Golda Meir

Facing Your Feelings

We all go through so many feelings every day, such as feeling tired, angry, happy, anxious, scared or mad. So often feelings come and go with no thought about them at all. Play "face your feelings" with children of all ages to help them identify and talk about their feelings. Get some paper and crayons or pencils, and get ready to draw. Each person draws a big circle representing their face. Pick one feeling from that day and draw it on your circle. When everyone has finished, they can share their pictures and the experience that created the feeling. The more we hear and understand each others' feelings, the better we know ourselves and the people we live with.

Getting in the Mood

Feelings come and go in 15 to 30 seconds, but moods can last for days. Everyone knows what it means to be in a good mood or a bad mood. But we don't always understand how our mood affects those around us; it can actually create a good or bad feeling in the home. Have fun dramatically acting out first a bad mood, then a good mood. Set a timer for 15 minutes, and everyone act out a bad mood: being judgmental, noncompliant, hostile, withdrawn, mopey, sulking, righteous. When the timer rings, everyone switch to acting out a good mood for 15 minutes: being helpful, attentive, generous, sweet, happy, caring, energetic, pleasant, patient, and so on. Discuss what it felt like to create these moods. Then discuss what it felt like to be around others with different moods.

Managing Anger

When children are very angry, they might feel like getting even. This is a normal feeling, so why not encourage your child to get this feeling out in a peaceful way. Take out a piece of paper and have them write down what they think the person deserves to have happen to them, based on what they did. When your children are finished writing, have them read the list out loud. Usually the severity of the punishments will make them laugh. After they have calmed down a little, discuss ways they might go about telling that person how they felt. Parents get angry too. Why not do the same exercise, but instead of reading the list out loud, simply crunch it up and throw it away. Then, tell the person you were angry at how you felt.

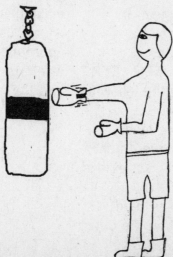

Responding to Difficult Feelings

Sometimes, when we see someone we care about hurt, mad, or unhappy, there is an urge to "fix it" instead of listening to the feelings expressed. Here's a game that will show everyone the difference between "fixing it" and listening. On index cards or pieces of paper, write the following sayings on one side:

Don't be mad.

Don't worry.

They didn't really mean it.

You should be happy.

Oh, it's not that bad.

and on the other side write "fix it." On other papers write the following saying on one side:

Sounds like you are mad.

I guess you are worried, huh?

That must have hurt your feelings.

You seem happy.

That must have been hard.

and the word "listen" on the other.

Fold the individual papers up and put them in a hat. Everyone picks a slip of paper and reads it to themselves. The oldest person makes up a situation that would make them feel mad, worried, happy, etc. Anyone who thinks they have an appropriate response on their slip of paper can say it. The person making up the scene then tells the group how the response would make them feel, and whether a "fix it" or "listen" response was more appropriate for them. Anyone who wants to can make up a situation and the game can continue.

I'm a Boy, Nothing Hurts Me

Boys get their feelings hurt too, but they are often too afraid of losing their masculinity to say something about it. Here's a game to show them that everyone has hurt feelings. This game works much better if there is one adult male playing. One person starts out by saying, "It makes me feel good when…," then adds one experience. The next person says another thing that makes them feel good and it keeps going until nobody can think of anything else to say. Sometimes it's fun to keep count of just how many sentences the group can add. Next, start off with the sentence, "It hurts my feelings when…," and everyone adds as much as they can to that. Lastly, start a sentence with, "It makes me feel bad when…" Each person add to it again. Just hearing that other people feel the same in a similar situation will make everyone feel that it's alright to express their feelings.

Releasing Difficult Feelings with Playdough

Buy or make a big bucket of playdough. This playdough is going to be used to help express the maddest, angriest, most jealous feelings each person might have. Take a piece of playdough and make it into a shape that fits the feeling you feel, then squeeze, hit, squish, throw, or step on the playdough. Use sound effects if it feels right. After a while you may even find yourself laughing. If children do this once, don't be surprised if they ask you for the tub of playdough again. It's also fun to join in with someone by making shapes and squeezing the playdough along with the person, encouraging their expression. This activity shows how sometimes difficult feelings can be transformed into more positive feelings when they are expressed freely.

Learning to Respond Well

Things happen to all of us that hurt, and we want to say something, but somehow we can't. Everyone think of, or make up, a situation that would be difficult to respond to: a group of kids called me a name, a teacher said I would have to stay after school, my boss fired me, my mom yelled at me. Write the situation on a piece of paper and put it into a hat. Each person will then pick a situation out of the hat. Go around and let each person read the situation out loud and say what they would do. If they don't know what they would do, they can say "help" and others can offer their ideas. Hearing how to respond to a certain situation may give children the courage to do it when the situation occurs.

The Benefit of Tears

Crying is an important part of letting a sad feeling out. So often people are afraid to cry because they don't want to seem vulnerable. Boys are often taught that only girls cry, which is untrue. Crying, like laughing, is a part of every person's life. If a child thinks it's acceptable to cry, they will let their feelings out instead of bottling them up inside. The next time you need to cry, don't run into another room; instead, let your children see you crying and tell them why you are sad. They will learn how to be compassionate and at the same time feel that crying is OK.

Entertaining Dinner Conversations

During a Friday night dinnertime, have a friendly competition involving the feelings people had during the week. Pick a feeling and ask "What was the most (fun, scary, sad, angering, happy, embarrassing) experience this week?" Everyone tell a true story from the week. Then take a family vote to determine the winner in each category. Making this a Friday night tradition will help the whole family be more attentive to their feelings throughout the week so they will have stories to tell. In fact, you will probably find the stories become more entertaining as the tradition continues.

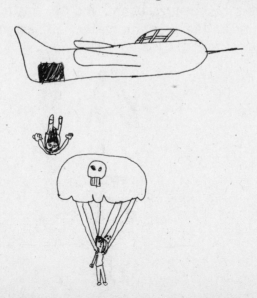

Feeling Ashamed

The word "shame" has a feeling of humiliation or embarrassment attached to it. As parents, we don't want our children feeling ashamed of themselves. We want them to learn from mistakes, and discover how to do something better or different the next time. Instead of feeling guilt and worthlessness, we want to help them find ways to fix what they have done so they can feel good about themselves. So, next time your child ruins a sibling's report, runs his bike into your car by accident, burns his finger on a pan you just told him to stay away from, or wets his pants at school, and you see that look of shame on his face or in his actions, let him express his feelings before you say anything. Help him think of ways he can make the situation better. Tell him you still love him.

Active Listening

In a family, some people feel they are helpful by solving problems and giving advice. Really, we can be most helpful if we just listen to the feelings of the person who has the problem as they talk through their options. This is a listening exercise. Get a partner. One partner thinks of a problem they have at work, school, or home. The other person listens to the story. The listener repeats back what they hear. Keep listening, don't ask questions, and keep repeating back to the person what you are hearing exactly as you hear it. Don't give advice and don't offer solutions. Let the speaker talk until they come up with some of their own ideas. Switch roles. If you think someone is asking you for advice, the best thing to do is to ask them if they want advice or if they just want you to listen.

What Is Failure?

Failure is not doing as well as you want at something; it is not making a team, it is feeling that you can't do anything right, it is the opposite of success. Standards for children are high these days, causing many children to feel they just aren't good enough. What can you do to make sure your child feels encouraged to try, without being afraid of failing? Watch the things your child does and praise them for the positive things you see. You can teach your child through your attitude that life contains both failure and success. Childhood is about trying many times and not always getting it right. Children should not expect to be good at everything. These comments help, but they can't always protect your child from feeling they have failed. When the feeling comes up, just listen to it until you remember how it feels. Then they will know you understand.

Putting Anger Behind You

Sometimes it's easier to get angry than it is to get "un-angry." Help your children learn how to de-fuse themselves. Have everyone write a letter to someone they are angry at, or towards whom they have built up resentment. Write all that you feel. Don't worry, because nobody will ever read this letter. This letter is for you. Take at least 20 minutes to write. When you are all done, get the letter writers together. As you each rip your letter into little pieces, enjoy the feeling and the sound of getting something off your mind. You might want to burn all the ripped up pieces in a fireplace. Sometimes, just writing feelings down helps a person feel better, and sometimes the bad feelings even go away. Once children have done this once, encourage them at other times to do it again when they feel angry at someone.

Dance the Feeling

Clear a large space of furniture, and select a surface you can pretend is a drum. Taking turns drumming. Let the drummer create rhythmic patterns that express one of the following feelings: joyful, scared, silly, somber, angry, tense, peaceful. The drummer announces the chosen feeling, then everyone moves to the beat in the spirit of that feeling. Let everyone have a chance to drum, being creative in expressing all the possible emotions one at a time.

Being Afraid

All parents personally feel their child's pain when they come home from school and say one of the following: "The school bully keeps pushing me and I'm afraid to go to school," "My best friend is spreading rumors and I'm afraid to say anything," "I have a report due tomorrow and I'm afraid to read it in front of the class." Children do have their fears. Here are some things you can do to help your child when they are feeling afraid.

- Listen to them and try to understand their fear.
- Brainstorm all the possible approaches to dealing with the fear. Write down every idea they come up with and work together on a plan.
- Role play (they play themselves and you play whoever else is involved) what your child is going to do, so they have a chance to practice and feel comfortable before facing the fear.
- Encourage whatever steps they take toward dealing with their fears.
- Tell a story from your own life when you felt afraid.

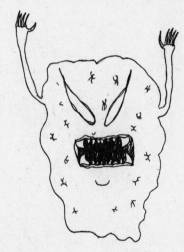

Expressing Feelings Colorfully

Get out a box of crayons, some markers, and a large sheet of paper for each person. Everyone think about their day. Make a big outline shape, such as a heart, circle, square, or diamond. Inside the circle, color an abstract design, or anything you want that expresses one of the feelings you had that day. Use color, shape, movement, and line to express that feeling. When everyone is done, look at each other's drawings and talk about them if you want to.

Understanding Your Anger

If you are feeling anger, it means there's an underlying problem. Here's a way to discover the problem under the anger. Put each one of the following problem statements on separate index cards:

- There's something I'm doing I don't want to do.
- There's something happening that I don't like.
- There's something I need that I'm not getting.
- There's something I'm getting that I don't want.
- There's something I'm not doing that I need to do.

Place the cards face down under a towel. The first person reaches around under the towel and pulls out a problem card, then answers the following three questions:

1. What's it like for you when you feel this way?
2. How do you act when this happens to you?
3. What's an example of this problem?

The next person then picks a problem card and answers the three questions. So often, we think someone else is the cause of the anger. But once we start to see anger as an indicator of a problem, then we can stop for a moment and start looking for the problem.

Communication

If a family were a building, communication would be the foundation that allows the building to stand through all sorts of bad weather. When there is good communication within a family, problems get solved, ideas get heard, feelings are expressed, and intimacy grows. When good communication is at work, love will always underlie the message, even when opinions differ.

"How can we communicate love? I think three things are involved: We must reach out to a person, make contact. We must listen with the heart, be sensitive to the other's needs. We must respond in a language that the person can understand. Many of us do all the talking. We must learn to listen and to keep on listening."
—Princess Pale Moon

Trying to Understood

Communication is people expressing their thoughts and feelings to each other. In order for communication to work, the thoughts and feelings have to be heard and understood. It's not as easy as it sounds. However, if you practice communication skills, hearing and understanding become easier. Here's a way to practice. Sit together in a circle. Each person gets five minutes to talk about anything they want, like school, work, hobbies, or problems. If you're not sure what someone is saying, ask a question. Don't move on to the next person until the person speaking feels heard and understood.

69

Feel Good and Feel Bad Words

Some words feel good, like "thank-you," "I love you," "what a great decision," and "you're so smart." Other words hurt, like "you idiot," "what's wrong with you?" or "can't you do anything right?" You might want to call them "up words" and "down words." Play this game. One person says some up words or down word phrases, then each person expresses how that word or phrase would make them feel. Go around the circle with each person thinking of the up followed by the down words, and then everyone join in with their feelings. Think of as many feelings as you can for each set of words. After this game, make it a family goal to use "up" words to build people up instead of "down" words that will tear them down. If someone uses "down" words at home, make sure to point out how feelings are hurt. You may even want to say, "No down words in this family."

Finding Out What Someone Means

Here's a fun game to play to find out what someone means when they say something. One person starts with a simple statement like "I like tomatoes," "I don't want to go to school," "I wish I could fly," "I like nice people." Everyone else take turns asking questions to learn more about what the person means. Start all the questions with "does that mean...?" The answering person says only yes or no. When it is obvious exactly what the person meant, move on to the next person. Don't be surprised if this takes a while. Really understanding one another can take time.

Speaking Eyeball to Eyeball

So often we talk to each other from across the room. We yell for the kids to do their homework, we expect them to hear us, and are mad when they don't. Today, try to speak every word while looking at each other "eye to eye." Get on your knees if talking to your child, stand on a stool if someone is taller. Make a game out of it. Expect amazing results; everyone you speak to just might hear and respond!

Letting the Young Feel Big

Do you remember what it was like to be a child, always looking up to the adults when you talked? Have fun reversing roles. The tall person sits on the ground and the smaller person stands as you have a conversation. Talk about anything you want. Does the new positioning affect the conversation in any way?

Children Taking the Initiative

Take one hour from a weekend day or an evening when everyone is home. During this time, the children get to start all conversation while the adults are responsive and receptive to what the children are saying. Offer help and encouragement if needed. Practicing initiating communication skills will give your child more confidence when speaking with other people.

Communicating without Words

How well can members of your family get their point across without words? The object of this game is to get someone to communicate something using only gestures, grunts, physical contact, or sign language; anything but words! Make the action simple, like opening the front door, pouring a glass of milk, putting a coat and boots on, writing a note, etc. One person does the gesturing while the others figure out what action is desired. Try to communicate the action without using physical props to actually perform the action. Switch roles frequently and try to get more creative with the actions as the game goes on.

Practicing Listening Skills

We practice many things: playing sports, reading, musical instruments, foreign languages, etc. Isn't it just as important to practice people skills? Children learn by example and by experience, so here's a way to give them both in a listening game. One person talks, the other person listens. First, the person listens using bad listening skills (look away from the person speaking, appear distracted or preoccupied, fiddle with something, interrupt, show no interest). Then the person listens using good listening skills (make eye contact, use occasional head nods, make brief comments on the subject the person is talking about, lean forward, look interested). The listener can spend two minutes listening poorly, then two minutes listening well. Make sure everyone has a turn. The people not playing the game should watch. It's entertaining to observe the poor listening skills so obviously demonstrated!

Family Discussion Box

After a family meal, or sometime when everyone is together, have each person write one idea of something they would like the whole family to talk about. It could be any kind of topic in the news, a topic being learned at school, vacation options, how to deal with a school bully, a moral issue, or anything a family member wants to discuss. All ideas get folded up and put into a box. Pick one idea and have a ten minute family conversation, practicing good listening, respect of other peoples' opinions and ideas, and not interrupting. If everyone enjoys it, pick one each night. Set aside an ideas box to which ideas can be added at any time. When going on a car trip, make sure to bring the discussion box along.

Talking Something Through

Sometimes it's not easy to get feelings and thoughts out in the first five sentences of speaking, especially if something is bothering you. Many people need to feel relaxed and listened to in order to talk comfortably. Give one person at a time the opportunity to follow the thread of their own thoughts. The talker picks anything that bothers them at this time, and then takes the time to talk about it. While the talker is between thoughts, listeners can breathe and practice patience. The talker decides when they are done talking. Everyone may not get a chance to talk because one person may need a lot of time, but be sure to schedule another the gathering so everyone gets a chance.

Time to Think

Giving a person time to think about what you've said to them is a wonderful gift. Thinking takes time. What would you like another person in the family to think about? Write that person a note or ask them in person to think about your idea, concern, or question. "Would you think about...going shopping with me later...where you want to go on vacation next year...doing your chores earlier in the day...me going to the prom...spending some time with me?" After a while has passed, find out if the person has thought about it, or if they need more thinking time. If you have been asked to think about something, set a time that day or the next to discuss your thoughts. If a child needs to talk, and you are too busy right then, it is very important that you say, "I want to listen to you but I can't right now, can we talk at 8:oo?" Then make sure you follow through; at 8:oo approach your child for that talk.

Letter Writing Night

It's so nice to get a letter in the mail. To help children learn the joy they can give others by sending letters, have a family letter writing night. Keep a basket full of paper, stationery, and cards to use on letter writing night. Turn on nice music, have cookies and milk and enjoy each other. Let everyone know if there is someone you know who is sick or going through a hard time, in case they want to write or draw pictures for that person. You may want to have a "letter" calendar for everyone's use. Write in friends' and relatives' birthdates. Write who each person sends a letter to, and on what date they send it. When letters are received, write that on the calendar also. Give the younger kids an older partner to help them with spelling and ideas.

Problem Solving in Different Styles

Does your family have a style of communication?
Here are a few possibilities:
- The mouse style, which includes crying, whining, moping, and begging.
- The monster style, which includes yelling, intimidating, and threatening.
- The direct style, which includes simply telling or asking without buffing things up or watering things down.

Starting with the mouse style, take the following problem and solve it as mice: The president is coming for dinner, the house is a mess, there is no food, and all the laundry is dirty. After you've experienced the futility of being mousy, then solve the same problem as monsters. Just before the monsters start to wipe each other out, try solving the problem using direct communication.

Voices by Mail

There is nothing quite as heartwarming as a cassette tape full of little voices singing, telling stories, reading poems, or sharing memories. Decide as a family who you would all like to send a tape like this to, and what will be on it. Put one of the kids in charge of actually getting the recordings from each person, or do it together one night as a group. It is also possible to make copies of this tape and send it to many people. Give each person a chance to sign their name to the package that gets mailed out.

Response Time

Any time you can find the opportunity, encourage your child to think about something. Here's how it works. Look for an opening in any conversation you might have with your child where they have asked a good question, need your opinion on something, or have a problem that they aren't sure how to handle. Respond like this: "I need a few minutes to think about that, so I'm just going to be quiet. Why don't you take a few minutes to think about it, too, and then we'll tell each other our thoughts." This kind of interaction shows your child that you value their ideas and thoughts.

Touch

One of the first experiences a baby has is the feeling of arms surrounding her, the sound of a heartbeat, and the touch of skin as she lay bonding with her parents. Touch is a profoundly basic need, essential for all of us to grow and thrive from the cradle to the grave. It has the ability to communicate a connectedness and caring without one word being said. Family is the primary and most important place where we learn the value of giving and receiving affection through touch.

"Surely even those immune from the world...
need the touch of another."
—Eudora Welty

Stress Release

When you see a family member looking stressed and emotionally strained, ask them if you can take some of their stress away. Place your entire hand on an area of the body, like the shoulders, back, head, or upper arms, for at least one minute. Wherever you have placed your hand is where the person can concentrate on relaxing their muscles. Tell them to take deep breaths as they imagine all the stress going out through your hands. Do this voluntarily when you see someone has had a bad day.

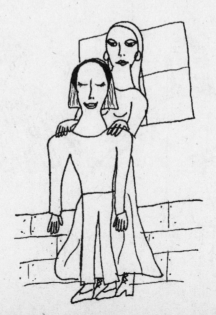

Rub a Hand

Who likes to have their hands massaged? Get a partner. One person closes their eyes and puts their hands out to be touched. The person touching experiments with different kinds of touch: tickle, push, rub, scratch, or squeeze. Once the person getting the hand massage identifies a touch they like, continue the massage for five or ten minutes, then switch. If you want to make it feel even more wonderful, massage a little vegetable oil into the hand.

Group Hug

Group hugs are a lot of fun, especially for children. Parents are used to group hugs if they have more than one child! Take some time before bed one night, or before everyone leaves in the morning, and have a group hug. Start with the biggest person standing in the center, with everyone else in a small circle around them. On the count of three, they get a nice long hug from everyone at the same time. Each person gets to be in the center of a group hug. It might be so much fun that everyone will want to do it every day.

Touching on Peace

Peace in the world starts with peace in the family. Remember the song "Reach Out and Touch Somebody's Hand"? Family can be the place where we learn to reach out towards others. Find time to have a peace circle. Hold each other's hands and close your eyes for a few minutes. Think good thoughts about your family, your friends, and the world's people. Moments like this remind children of the values their family holds dear.

Earth Touch

The earth touches us in many ways: through our eyes as we see the changing colors of autumn or the swelling of ocean waves; through our hands as we touch the water of a cool mountain stream; through our nose as we smell spring flowers; through our ears as we listen to birds or the wind. Go outside together and take a short walk. Walk silently together feeling the wind, hearing the birds, seeing the beauty around you. When you get home, talk about how the earth touches and inspires each of your lives.

Your Favorite Feel

Many things become our favorites because they feel good: a sweatshirt, pillow, pet rabbit, soft brush or lotion. Have a hunt where everyone has ten minutes to bring back to the group one to three things that they like simply because they like the way they feel. Once everyone returns from the hunt, let each person pass their items around to be felt by everyone. As the item is being felt, have the person say why they like it so much.

Imagine Life without Touch

Storytelling is fun for everyone, especially if each person gets to add to the story. Start the story with, "Once upon a time there was a land where nobody touched each other." Each person contributes to the story by adding a few lines. Make the story as fun and imaginative as possible. Keep it going for as long as someone has a story to tell.

Massage Train

Have everyone sit in a line like a train. Begin to massage the neck and shoulders of the person sitting in front of you. After five minutes, everyone turn and face the opposite direction and begin massaging the neck and shoulders of the person now in front of you. This is a great way to make sure no one is left out; everyone can laugh and enjoy themselves together. Make sure to let each other know how great the massage feels.

91

Pressure Points

There are pressure points on our hands and feet which, when pressed, can help free up energy and relieve stress and anxiety. Copy onto a large piece of paper the two pictures below, or have someone teach everyone to locate the points on their own hands and feet. Pick a partner and have fun while you locate the points on your partner. Follow the numbers and directions below.

1. Pinch and rub big toe using thumb on bottom of toe and forefinger on top.
2. Pinch both sides of ankle.
3. Pinch from top and bottom of foot the big bone below big toe.
4. Pull and pinch each toe one at a time.

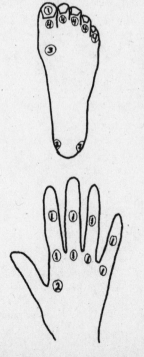

1. Each finger joint is pinched (by thumb and forefinger) pressuring the joint from the palm side and back side at the same time.
2. Pinch in the same way the point between thumb and forefinger.
3. When finished, wrap free hand around thumb and one finger at a time, holding each finger for 30 seconds.

Earth Hug

When was the last time you took the time to lie on the ground? Take a blanket outside and do it today. Close your eyes and let your body sink into the earth. Lie quietly for fifteen minutes. This works wonders after a family argument, a tense day at work or school, when a decision has to be made, or when you just want to feel life for a while.

Learning to Say No

Nobody likes the job of telling their children about bad touch. As a parent, you might feel you are making your child's world a little darker by telling them that there are bad people in the world who could hurt them. So what do you do? There are many pamphlets and books written on this subject, and presentations given from pre-school on. Here are a few of the most important points to remember:

- Open communication is the most important thing. Listen to your child, and don't sound shocked at things they tell you, or they will stop telling you. Your child has to trust that you will love them no matter what they say, or no matter what might have happened.

- Talk about their bodies openly and often so they don't feel embarrassed. Teach your child that nobody has the right to touch them unless they want to be touched. Point out that they can tell anybody, at any time, that they don't want to be touched, even if it's only a hug.

- Work on trust in the family so you can always believe your child. If they feel uncomfortable in any way, something is not right. It is your job to investigate and protect them no matter what the cost.

Experience the Senses

When a person is blindfolded, they can experience touch, taste, smell, and sound to a greater degree. Get out enough scarves to blindfold half of your family members. Each person gets a partner that can see. That partner is going to lead the blindfolded person on a sensory tour. Be creative and include things like feeling running water, tasting something sweet, sour, warm, or cold, and touching tree bark, grass, or a soft bunny. Put things under their nose and see if they can guess what it is by the smell. Do this activity slowly, with a sense of wonder and adventure. This is not a time to play tricks on each other. Rather, it is a time to learn trust. Switch roles often so everybody gets a chance.

Part Three:
About Others

Caring

Caring is a way of living, it's not optional within the family or within the world. A family is like a garden in many ways: we all grow at different paces, we need the nutrients of love and connectedness to survive, and we need weeds removed and new seeds planted every now and then. The greatest gift a family can give its members is the knowledge that everyone is responsible to care for the family garden as well as the world's garden. Each person needs to put time into its upkeep, to weed once in a while, and to do their share of watering so that each person can grow into themselves in a supportive environment.

"A garden dies quickly without a loving gardener to keep it alive."
—May Sarton

Nurse Duty

Moms and Dads are expected to care for the sick children in the house. Why not teach children how to care as well? When a member of your family is sick, make up a "nurse duty" schedule. This schedule would give each family member certain hours each day to be responsible for making sure the sick person is cared for, has water to drink, something to read, someone to talk to if they want to talk, food, enough blankets, and help getting around. Emphasize to the children how good it feels to be cared for when not feeling well. When the child is sick, they can expect the same treatment from other family members. Children love to feel needed, and often they care very much, but don't know what to do to help. This will give them something they can do to show how much they care.

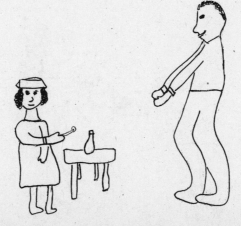

Post a Note

Empathy is feeling compassion for someone else; doing for them what you would like done for you if you were in the same situation. One small way to show you care is to post notes around the house for the person you feel needs support. Post one on the bathroom mirror so the first thing they see in the morning is your encouragement; post one on their cereal bowl so they eat with a smile on their face; post one on their car window, etc. Writing these notes only takes a few moments. The notes can simply read things like: "You can do it, be brave," "I love you, you're the best," "I'll be thinking of you today." You will only have to do this one time and your children will most likely want to participate in the fun; so put some markers in a small basket with a pile of Post-it notes and encourage everyone to post a few notes a week.

Thank-You

In a family, so many things are done each day that go unnoticed and unappreciated. Take some time today to have a thank-you ritual. Sit together and, focusing on one person in the family at a time, everyone begins to tell that person what they appreciate them for: "I appreciate you, (first name), because _____. Thank-you." Don't rush the thanks, it helps everyone feel good about their efforts and encourages cooperation in the future. Each person gets the chance to be the receiver of the appreciation.

While You're Away

Before you leave on a vacation or a weekend getaway, talk to your children about how they will feel about your absence. Tell them a story from your own childhood about when your parents went away. Make a cassette tape together with each child; read a story, recite a poem, laugh or sing songs. When your children feel lonely, they can put this tape on and remember that you cared how they would feel while you were gone. Model empathy whenever you can and your children will mirror it.

Watch and Wonder

You know the old saying, "You should not judge another until you have walked a mile in that person's moccasins." Well, here's your chance to imagine what another person's life is like. After all, the basis for empathy is being able to feel what another feels. You cannot feel what someone else feels unless you can imagine their life. Spend an hour one day together out in the city, at a park, or someplace where you will see people different from the people in your family. After you have had a little time to observe the people, sit together and each person make up a story about what they imagine another person's life is like.

Caring for Nature

Although nature is all around us, unavoidable and inescapable, we all take it for granted unless we pay attention to it, seeing its beauty. It's easier to care about something you have experienced, something that is special to you. We want our children to grow up caring about their world and gaining peace from the natural environment around them. Teach them to pay attention to nature by looking at it together. One day each week for a month, just before the youngest member's bedtime, everyone go out together to enjoy the moon. Night by night, watch it grow or diminish and change position in the night sky. Make up a story about the moon. One person can start it, with each person adding a few lines. Also, check a book out of the library that shows a map of the night stars. Learn and look for the constellations together. Then listen in silence to the night sounds and see if you can identify them.

Model Empathy

In order for a child to be empathetic, she must be able to understand another's emotions and be able to share them. This is not a skill a child will learn unless they see it often in the people around them. Here are a few things to do to make sure your child can recognize empathy:

- When your child has done something to hurt someone, avoid doing the same thing to your child as was done to the victim. Instead, focus your attention on the hurt child, and how they are feeling. Then have your child come up with something they can do to make the hurt child feel better.

- Whenever you see someone being empathetic, point it out to your child: how nice it was for a neighbor to bring dinner when she knew you were sick, or your appreciation when one of your children brings you a blanket because they think you're cold.

- Role play with your child when they tell you things that happen at school, like bullying, name-calling, or teasing. Ask them to pretend they were the child being teased and tell you how they would feel.

Watch TV Together and Talk About It

There are many shows on TV that depict family situations where people are living together and trying to get along. Pick one of these shows to watch together as a family. Talk about how the actors treat each other, and highlight scenes where they act with empathy toward another actor. Also, point out the places where the behavior is not empathetic. During the commercials, mute the sound and reenact a scene so that the people are treating each other with empathy. Most importantly, point out to your children that most things they see on television are not to be copied in real life. TV shows are often about conflict between people. There are very few shows about families getting along.

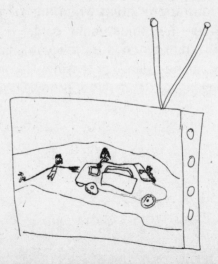

Your Child's World

There are many chances each day to show a child what empathy looks like. Take any of the following situations: the cereal your child loves is gone, he can't find his homework assignment, her best friend is moving or he hates his hair. We think our children should breeze through these simple problems, because we would breeze through them ourselves. But take a few minutes and imagine yourself as a child in the same predicament. Then, remember that not finding a homework assignment for them could feel like losing a big deal at work to you. After you have thought a moment, and can feel the importance of your child's problem, reflect back to them the feelings they might be having and be empathetic. They will learn from your example how to see something through another's eyes. What is simple and easily solved for some, is difficult for others. That is why listening and understanding are so important.

Friendship

Friends are like treasures placed in our lives, full of beautiful jewels and interesting artifacts. They bring new ideas to our minds, share in who we are and in who we are struggling to become, and walk, if only for a while, down life's path with us side by side. It's been said that you can choose your friends but you can't choose your family. It is a gift when a family chooses to be friends, remembering that to have a friend you must be a friend.

"A friend is one who knows all about you and likes you anyway."
—Christi Mary Warner

Being a Friend Means...

Talk to your children about what a friend is. Tell them about the friends you have, and why you like them. Listen as they tell you about the friends they have. Together write a book or card that talks about friendship. Title it something like, "What being a friend means to me," "The kind of friend I want," or "Friends are the best because..." Inside have your child write all their thoughts on the subject of friendship. As you create this book together, share all your own years of experience developing friendships, and give your child a chance to ask questions about friendship, and to tell you their problems with friends. This card or book should be saved, so that when a problem occurs—your child feels they don't like a certain friend any more, or their best friend doesn't like them—you can read through it together and remember what friendship is all about.

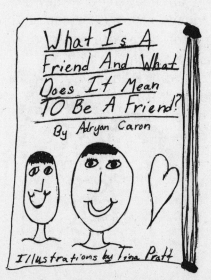

What Is A Friend And What Does It Mean TO Be A Friend?
By Adryan Caron

Illustrations by Tina Pratt

Building Friendships

Friendships are important at any age. Making friends is easy once you know how. The first step is deciding who you like to be around: who makes you laugh, says the right thing, is smart, never picks on you, or is just plain fun to be with? Help your child make a "Friends List" of the people they like. Next to the name, write the reasons that person is now a friend, or the reasons your child would like them to be a friend. Now comes the hard part, explaining that friendship has to be worked at: friends do things together, share experiences and enjoy similar things. If the person is already a friend, these things are happening; if they are not, talk together about ways to become friends with this person. You might set simple goals like talking to that person once each day, or asking them to eat lunch or to play a game. Following through with the ideas is not always easy, especially if your child is a little shy, so be encouraging and ask about daily progress. If it's very difficult for your child to make friends, you might get to know one of the parents of a child on the Friends List.

What's Wrong?

Some days are better than others. On the days when something happens that bothers us, it's a good idea to let it out in some way. Talking to someone is usually the best, but if that's not possible, teach your child to write it down. A shoe box with a hole cut in the lid could be decorated and given the honor of receiving the written complaints. This box could be placed at the entryway to the house. The idea is to see home as a peaceful place, a place where feelings can be expressed in whatever way possible, a place where family members are treated like friends. So, instead of taking out a bad day on a family member or on yourself, do the best you can to write it down and leave it at the door.

Help with Friend Problems

It's normal for kids to be friends one day and not the next, part of the group today and out of the group tomorrow. The good news is that kids usually resolve the issues, and are friends again in a matter of days. The best thing a parent can do is let children work through the problem themselves, so they can learn how relationships work. It is a good idea, however, to monitor (in a subtle way), the relationships your children have by listening to them talk about the situations that develop. When listening, simply repeat to your child the situation they have described as you understand it ("Sally said you weren't her friend anymore"); then sympathize with her feelings ("you must feel sad, I know Sally was your favorite friend"); suggest options ("have you tried talking to her, maybe you could call her on the phone and talk"); and tell similar stories about things that happened with you and your friends when you were your child's age.

Peer Pressure

Parents all dread the day their children begin to value their friends' thoughts and ideas more than their parents' views. It's called peer pressure, and it starts at about age seven, when kids are at school hearing and seeing what other kids say and do. Peer pressure can be good when it inspires your child to write a better story, attend more swim practices, or run for class president. It can be terrible if it inspires your child to take drugs, steal something, or pick on their brother or sister. Who your child chooses as a friend does influence the kind of person they become. So, if you want to keep track of who your child's friends are and what they are like, get to know them. Have a barbecue, potluck dinner, or picnic once every six months and invite your children's closest friends and their parents. Invite a friend when your family goes on an outing together. Volunteer at school so you can hear what is going on and interact on a weekly basis with the kids and their teachers. Try to keep track without seeming like a spy, or a judge of each friend's character. Forbidding your child to be friends with someone is not a good idea; instead, share your fears about the choices, attitude, and direction this child is choosing for their life. If you need help, talk to the school counselor, who will be happy to give you ideas.

A Friendly Debate

Learning how to have a friendly debate will help children have confidence in conversations. Get the family together to talk about or debate a subject that's of interest to everyone. It could be something silly like "birds are more intelligent than dogs," or it could be serious like "how to feed the homeless and get them off the streets," or it could be personal like "what would you do if you were suddenly poor?" The idea is to talk freely, listening to each person's ideas without one person doing all the talking. If you run out of things to say about one topic, try another. You will get to know each other better by talking and listening to each person's thoughts, feelings, and opinions. The more you know about each other, the closer you will feel as friends. Encourage your child to have a friendly debate with a few of their friends.

Build Friendship in Your Family

You know the old saying, "You can choose your friends but you can't choose your family"; well, it's possible to choose that your family will be friends. Think of the ways you interact with friends: sharing information, supporting each other and having fun together. With a little work, your family can contain all of these elements. Here are some ideas of ways to get it started:

- Take an interest in what is going on in each person's life by talking to each other about daily events.
- Ask specific questions. Instead of saying, "Did you have a good day?" ask "Did you do well on that test you were studying for?" or "How did the pot you were painting in art class turn out?"
- Dance while you do the dishes together.
- Take a walk in the rain.
- Share interesting things from the newspaper, a book you're reading, current events, or a comic strip the family could follow together.
- Encourage family discussions that the children can participate in.
- Ask questions to stretch the imagination "What if people lived on the moon?"
- Ask your child to teach you something they learned at school today.
- Have a pizza party, or a family letter writing night.
- Bring up old memories about your child, an event, or an experience your child is having.

Teach your children by example that friendship is built; it takes time and effort to have a good friend.

111

Rejected by the Clique

So often, when children come to their parents upset that they have been rejected by the "in clique," parents respond by telling their child one of the following: "You don't need those friends," "You are better than they are, just forget them," or "Find other friends who have the same values." Well, being part of a clique is part of adolescence, and it is very important to your child. Here are a few pointers to remember when your child struggles with this aspect of friendship.

- Help your child to learn how to be part of the group, rather than giving him reasons why he shouldn't.
- Don't fight battles for your child by confronting the other children or their parents. Listen to your child's feelings, then together come up with how your child might respond.
- Encourage your child to stand up for themselves. Your job is to stand by to give moral and emotional support.
- Allow your child to wear the clothes that the other kids are wearing. Being normal and not sticking out is important to preteens. Pick your battles: clothes and hair length or backpack style doesn't need to be on the list of things to argue about.
- Tell them stories about your life and friends, at their age. This is a good way to convey your values without being angry or preachy.

No matter what your child tells you, they do still value your opinion. Be careful not to get too emotional about the problem at hand, or you will make it very difficult for them to resolve the issue themselves, or to even admit problems to you in the future.

Respect

If respect is something we want to receive from others in our lives, it's something we must also learn to give. When we respect someone we regard them as worthy of our thoughtfulness. When the effort is made to respect another, the message is clear, "I see you and I value you."

"A life of goodness and decency begins with
the recognition of the infinite worth of
each and every human being."
—Wayne Dosick

Respect Privacy

It's important to establish rules that reflect the family's view on an individual's right to privacy. Get everyone together to make up a list of rules: knock on the door before entering, ask before borrowing something, don't open other people's mail, don't ask who someone just talked to on the phone, no eavesdropping. These rules will give children a guideline to follow, and will establish in their minds the idea that, even in a full house, people have privacy rights that need to be respected.

Treat Others with Respect

Children learn how to treat others by watching how adults treat them. It always helps to ask yourself the following question: "How would I handle the same situation if I were dealing with a guest or a friend?" In other words, if you want your child to come immediately, even though you see they are engrossed in a project, you might want to give them a few minutes of warning. Then, the next time they need you immediately and see you engrossed in a project, they will know how to deal with the situation. Children learn how to treat others with respect by watching how their parents interact with others. If you have an attitude that allows you to talk whatever way you want to a waiter, secretary or store clerk, your child will act the same way. Children learn about respect throughout their lives, so keep setting a good example.

Quiet in Public Places

It's not always easy for children to be quiet when you want them to. Here's a pretend game you can all play as a way of rehearsing an event. Do you expect to be in a doctor's or dentist's waiting room soon, or in a library, or visiting someone elderly, or having a family dinner in a restaurant? Pick a situation like one of the above and set up a pretend stage so everyone can act out the situation. Then start play acting whatever the real situation would be, using appropriate voices. Under many circumstances, speaking softly is a way of being respectful. It also helps to tell kids the reasons why quiet is appreciated under these circumstances.

Slow It Down

Do you ever feel like your children are going way too fast? Maybe you're at the mall and they are running through the store picking up everything, or you are going to visit a friend and they are bugging you to get organized to leave, or they are eating dinner so fast you are sure they'll choke. Here's a fun way to practice slowing down. Pick a night when everyone is home. One person starts out by calling out "SLOMO," and for one minute, everybody has to move in slow motion, continuing to do whatever they were just doing. Everyone resumes their normal activity

after the minute is up. After about five minutes of regular motion, someone else gets to call "SLOMO" and everyone slows down again. Keep this up as long as everyone is having fun. The object is to then take this behavior into situations where everyone is moving too fast. The word "SLOMO" will be a code word that everyone understands.

Cooperation

Part of the power of family is that there is a ready-made team! As most parents/coaches know, the challenge lies in creating team spirit and the desire to work together for a common goal. It is in the family where a child first experiences getting along with others, working together on something, having to share, and not always being first. We all learn to set aside individual needs for the needs of the group. Learning to cooperate will give your child a valuable tool for future success in school, relationships, and the working world.

"The nice thing about teamwork is that you always have others on your side.
—Margaret Carty

Stuck Together

Remember the old three-legged race where kids get tied together and have to run someplace moving their legs together? This game is a variation on it; it allows children to learn how to cooperate and work together, while at the same time laughing and having fun. Tie two children together at the elbows and the ankles so the children are standing side by side. Then, give them a chore to do. They have to talk about how they will do it, walk and move together, and decide which hand will do what. Prepare for loads of laughter as they negotiate the task. Cooperation means taking another person into consideration—what better way than to be stuck together!

Spring Cleaning

Have everyone take one day off to work together cleaning closets, drawers or the garage, in preparation for a garage sale. Each person should bring clothes, games, pictures, books, or whatever they don't want anymore, to a central location in the house. Before you have the sale, let each person in the family pick out the things they might want to keep from the items that other family members are giving away. After the family has a chance to "shop," plan a garage sale, or give what is left to a charity. This is a great way for younger children to acquire an older child's games or clothing, without feeling that they are getting it handed down to them without a choice.

Create a Mood

In your home, you have the opportunity to create many different moods. If classical music is playing, the mood feels different than it would if rock music were playing. A picnic doesn't have the same feeling as a candlelit dinner. Comedy night sets a different mood than a family political debate would. Use your creative juices, and as a group, pick a mood you would like to create for an evening. Then, plan the evening together. Decide what needs to be done and who will do it. When the evening arrives, make sure everyone cooperates, enjoying the mood that has been created. Plan an evening like this every once in a while so that each family member gets a chance to pick a new mood.

Family Garden

Pick a place in your yard to design a garden together. Each person could design a section picking the flower or vegetable they want to plant. It helps children if they can look at colored plant catalogues when deciding what they want to plant. That way they can see how the whole garden will look when it is finished. It's fun to have children write their names in the dirt with flower seeds. When the flowers bloom, they are so excited to see the piece of art they have created out of the letters of their name. You may even want to write the family's last name with flower seeds so everyone can get excited!

Quiet and Alone

When you live in a house with other people, it sometimes feels nice to be alone. Everyone needs to work together so that space and time can be created for each person to be alone. Of course, it may be impossible to be physically alone but it may be possible for each person to spend thirty minutes removed from one another in silence. This is a good time to think, read, write, or just relax, enjoying the peace and quiet. Turn off the phone, radio, stereo, and television. You may all like it so much that you'll want to pick a weekly time to repeat this.

Picture a Season

122

Working on a craft project, where everyone has to add something to the same piece of paper, gives kids the chance to practice many cooperation skills: they have to agree on the design, listen to each other's opinions, work together, and give up some of their preferences. Get together for a family walk to collect small objects you find outdoors: flowers, grasses, sand, seeds, pods, leaves, roots, dirt, bark, berries, stones. Take a few egg cartons along on the walk to put the found objects into. When you're back at home, all you'll need is a large posterboard and glue. Everyone works together to create one picture that will emerge from each person's contribution of found natural objects. There is no director; everyone must work together to create this grand nature collage.

Open to Change

Living involves changing and growing. If within the family we view change as what defines something that's alive, we will be planting the seed in our children's minds that change is an expected life adventure. Change then becomes a thrilling part of everyday life, something easily accepted as the norm. So, next time one of life's surprises arrives at your doorstep, open the door with enthusiasm.

"If we don't change, we don't grow.
If we don't grow, we are not really living."
—Gail Sheehy

Change What?

Everyone who lives in a family knows there are things to like and things not to like about family life. There will always be areas that need to change, like noise in the morning, having things disappear, someone monopolizing the phone, or a messy room. There will always be things we all hope never change, like bedtime hugs, afterschool cookies, or Sunday night dinner. Have everyone get together. Start with each person saying two things they don't want to change, followed by two things they do want to change. Make a list of the things people want to change. Think and talk about these things in a fun way, without arguing or blaming. Just remember, if everyone in the family liked the same things, life would be boring!

Change Is a State of Mind

Since everyone has to live together in the same home environment, and everyone agrees that it's worth the effort to make that home as fun a place to live as possible, consider the following:

- Post the list you all made in Activity 123 someplace where everyone can see it.
- Each person look at the list and think of some small thing they could do that would produce a positive change, such as lowering your voice, asking before borrowing, or picking up after yourself.
- Pick a day for everyone to make the small change they have thought about.

Note: Changing behavior is very difficult, so if you see someone making the effort, be sure to tell them what a good job they are doing!

Make a Pact

If the little changes in Activities 123 and 124 have made your home a more positive place, why not have a little celebration documenting the family's accomplishments and future goals. Make a pact with each other, a commitment to become the best you can be together. Start it like this, "We the people of the _____ family, agree to do our best to make our family as loving and respectful as we can..." Feel free to add whatever statement or goals you have as a group. Everyone sign or initial the paper starting with the youngest of the group. Who said families couldn't be run like a community club!

Change Is an Adventure

Life is about changes. Few things stay the same. If children learn to see change as an adventure, a challenge, and an opportunity to learn they will have the confidence to try new things. Kids are encouraged to practice sports, and musical instruments to get better at them. Why not practice doing familiar things in different ways to get better at change? Practice changing routines, and practice venturing into the unknown. Here are some ideas:

- Go to a place nobody in your family has ever been.
- Pick an activity that nobody has done, like camping, skiing, or bowling. Then do it.
- Research a subject nobody in the family knows anything about.
- Rearrange an existing family schedule.
- Invite a new person to your house.

A family that is not afraid to venture out and try new things has a life of its own. This kind of attitude creates brave children who are interested in what life has to offer.

Charting Process

Too often, children get the idea from parents and society that they are expected to do things perfectly. A goal is set and the goal is either reached or not. Today is a good day to start talking about the word "progress." Progress is the series of steps a person takes walking toward a goal or a change that they want to make. Kids need to learn how to make steps of progress. Help your child select a goal they have, or a change they are ready to make. Draw a stairway with your child and write something on each step that will help your child reach the desired goal or change. Put a sticker on each step as progress is made. Be enthusiastic with each step, and be sure to celebrate when the goal is reached!

Rag Doll Game

"Out of sight, out of mind" is what happens sometimes with rules we set up as parents. Play this game with your kids to illustrate the frustration of having children who act a certain way in front of the caregiver, then change their behavior when the caregiver is out of sight:

The caregiver acts like a rag doll waiting for the doll maker (the child) to put them in a desired pose. The doll maker (child) puts the doll (caregiver) in whatever pose they want to. The doll holds the position as long as the doll maker is looking at the doll. The rest of the group gives the doll maker things to do, like stack some blocks or read a page from a book. Every time the doll maker turns or looks away, the doll can relax, and the doll maker has to go back and put the doll back into position. This is a fun way for kids to feel the pressure caregivers feel when a child doesn't follow set rules, and the caregiver has to pay constant attention. Next time you are busy making dinner, remind them of the rag doll game!

Finding New Things Around You

Take a walk around the neighborhood together with your children. The task is to look for things you have never seen before. See if it's possible to discover at least one thing no one has ever noticed before. If you can't walk around your neighborhood together, send everyone off to school, work, errands, etc., with the same investigative assignment: to notice the things in their daily environment, and find something never seen before. After dinner, each person can tell what they found.

The Old vs. the New

Let the children in your family pick some activity they do well, and then teach it to the adults: playing a tune on the piano, hitting a baseball, playing dress-up, creating a craft project or writing poetry. Give your child a chance to teach you; it will build their sense of self-worth. Adults, take some time to think...are you willing to let your children teach and guide you?

Rubbing Stone

Every person has some behavior they don't like: yelling in the house, being jealous of someone, sucking a thumb or swearing. If your child has a behavior you want changed, try a different approach. Instead of demanding the behavior be changed, talk with them about the behavior. Find out if they like having that behavior, or if they want to take steps to stop it. Tell them you know it will be hard, and you want to help them. Go look for a stone together; a polished store-bought stone, or one found in your own yard will do. This stone is to be carried around in a pocket or pouch. Whenever the child starts to feel like doing the behavior they want to stop, they should be instructed to rub the stone and think positive thoughts and tell themselves they can stop that behavior. After a while, when your child feels they don't need the stone anymore, take them to a lake or stream where they can throw the stone away. As they throw the stone, let them yell, "I'm done with _____!" It is important that you acknowledge and support any efforts made.

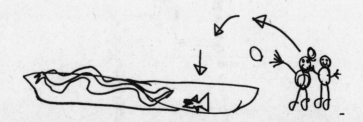

Cook a Meal Together

Broaden your horizons by experiencing another culture. Pick an ethnic meal to cook together. Research menu possibilities and decide who will cook each dish. Give the children the job of finding a story, song, or poem to share. A brief history of the country and its traditions would be fun, or go all-out and come in costume!

Seeds of Change

It takes time for new behaviors to grow. Get a seed of any kind and plant it in a pot. The seed represents the desired change. Explain to the child how the new behavior has to take root, just like the seed. The child can water the seed every day, and at the same time work towards making their own change. By the time green leaves are showing, the child should be on their way to changing their own behavior. The plant can also be a reminder to the caregiver that growth happens over time; just as the seed grows slowly, so does the child.

Manners

Manners are simply specific behaviors that reflect an awareness of other people's feelings. Learning the socially accepted and expected behavior that is respectful of others' feelings takes time and effort. The learning happens each day within the family as actions are modeled and values are talked about. A child with manners can confidently interact with others in a way that will attract positive feedback, and it is this positive feedback that will encourage the mannerly action to continue.

"Manners are a sensitive awareness of the feelings of others. If you have that awareness, you have good manners, no matter what fork you use."
—Emily Post

Top Ten Manners

When it comes to manners, the job of defining and teaching them is up to you, the parent. Most importantly, children will copy you, so now is the time to brush up on any rusty skills of your own! Make a list of ten manners you want each of your children to have. Together, pick one manner to work on each week for the next ten weeks. Write that manner someplace the child will see often. When you add a new manner, make sure to keep giving positive feedback for the old one, so that it will continue. Children learn good manners very quickly when they get smiles and pats on the back from all the adults around them. If you need help with your list, many of the following activities list age appropriate manners.

Imagine Life with No Manners

This is a group storytelling activity about what life would be like if nobody had any manners! Have the oldest person begin the story with, "Once upon a time, there was a land where nobody had good manners." Being as imaginative as possible, each person adds a bit to the story about this land where there is no respect or consideration for other people at home, around the table, at work, on the playground, at the mall, on the phone, etc. Let the story go on as long as everyone is having fun. Talk about the bad-mannered land afterward and how the people could have acted with more consideration for each other.

Simon Says Please

Here's a fun game to play to get into the "please" and "thank-you" habit. Someone gets to be leader first. Instead of saying "Simon Says" the leader says "please" before each command and "thank-you" after a command is followed. Commands should be simple, like "please touch your nose," "please close your eyes," "please turn around in a circle." Just like in Simon Says, if the leader gives a command without saying "please," and the player follows that command, the player is out. The leader is out if he fails to say "thank-you" after a command is followed. If this happens, someone who is already out gets to be leader. Keep playing—the longer you play, the stronger the habit.

Greetings

A friendly greeting is one of the simplest and most appreciated good manners a child can have. Children have different abilities based on their age: a three to five year old can be expected to look at the person, say hello, and possibly shake their hand; a six to nine year old can handle a simple introduction like, "Mom this is Pete, Pete this is my mother." By ten years old, a child can introduce friends to the adults present and tell them something about their friend, like how they met or something the friend likes to do. If nobody introduces the child (eight to twelve years), they should know how to introduce themselves to the adults present. It is customary to call adults Mr. or Ms. unless the adult tells the child to call them by another name. Practice greeting people by role playing. You might try showing your child how to move from a greeting into a conversation. Make sure to tell them how wonderful they are when you see them giving a friendly greeting.

Mealtime Manners

Here are a few mealtime manners that most people follow:

- Asking for food to be passed
- Proper use of utensils
- Keeping elbows off the table
- Asking to be excused
- Remaining until all are done eating
- Chewing with mouth closed
- Sitting still
- Leaving hand in lap
- Waiting for the cook to sit down before you start eating
- Saying please and thank-you

Manners have to be practiced to be learned; they also have to be modeled. Younger children may not be able to do all the above manners; however, as they watch other family members' behavior at the table they will learn from them. Make a list of all the mealtime manners your family wants to follow. Put that list up near the dining table. It's a good idea to pick one manner per week to work on together. Say the manner before dinner, and let each person monitor themselves. If, after the meal, the person feels they have succeeded with that manner, they can give themselves a star.

Don't Say Don't

Since you have decided to teach your children better manners, why not communicate your lessons to them in a mannerly way? Using negative commands like "don't put your elbows on the table," "don't speak on the phone like that," or "don't leave your stuff around the house," doesn't work, because the child is likely to get defensive. Here's a new approach. Using positive commands, you can direct the child toward the positive manners. For example: "I like it when you answer the phone with a stronger, clearer voice like this," "try holding your fork like this, it looks better," "please look at me when you are speaking to me," or "it would be nice if you could greet Grandma at the door." The next time you feel the word "don't" creeping up, take a deep breath and rewrite the old script. By changing your parenting style, you will be modeling better manners.

Openings to Talk

It's hard to learn conversation skills: when to listen, when to talk, and when it isn't interrupting to jump into a conversation. So often, kids have so much to say, that they get mad when one of their siblings interrupts and starts telling their story. They want everyone to wait for a long time until everything has been told. Well, that can be frustrating for others who have also participated in the event, because they want to contribute to the conversation. In a game-like setting, practice having a conversation where there are spaces left in the conversation for someone to jump in with their ideas. The adults can point out good places to jump in by saying the word "now." Point out when a person has been talking for too long without letting someone else jump in. Practice this game often, as it develops a wonderful sense of how to listen and contribute to a conversation.

Signal an Interruption

Kids have a tendency to interrupt their parents in all sorts of different situations. Instead of correcting them in front of others and embarrassing them, try making up a signal to use when they are interrupting: a hand to your ear, a snap of your fingers or a finger to your mouth. Whenever they start to interrupt, give them the signal. This could also work for other manners you are working on. It's just a small reminder that helps your child remember the behavior they are trying to master. By not embarrassing your child in front of others, you also model for him how to respect another's feelings.

Words We Use

Simple words and simple rules can go a long way in teaching manners that will last a lifetime. Make a list of the following phrases and rules; talk about them, then post the list someplace where everyone can see it.

Words: Please, Thank-you, No thank-you, You're welcome, Excuse me, How are you? Fine thanks, how are you? It's nice to meet you.
Rules: Speak when spoken to, No whispering or telling secrets about others, Avoid making insults, Use proper English, If you can't say something nice don't say anything at all.

Encourage children whenever you hear or see them using one of the above words or rules. Keep telling them how much people like to be around children with good manners.

Phone Talk

A great way to teach good phone manners is by playful practice with a tape recorder or unplugged phone. Children love feeling they have learned something well. If they practice the words to use when answering the phone, how to respond to the person on the other end of the line, and how to take messages, they will be confident and excited about using their good manners on the phone. Talk together about what would be polite phone responses. Get out the tape recorder and practice phone conversations. Parents can role play different conversations the child is likely to encounter. Make sure to have a pad of paper handy so the child can practice taking down information the caller gives them. Listen to the tape together and give lots of positive feedback.

Make a rule that adult calls take precedence over children's calls. This may seem unfair to the children, but it will teach them something about respect for elders, and also keep a sense of order with incoming calls.

Giving and Accepting Compliments

Teach your children to look for good things in other people: a nice outfit, pretty smile or a job well done. Everyone appreciates it when they receive a nice compliment. Sit down with your child and think of a compliment they could give a teacher, sibling, parent, or friend. Encourage them to say that nice thought to somebody and report back to you how that person responded. When receiving a compliment, the response should always be "Thank-you very much." It's rude to make up excuses about yourself, or say negative things back. Accept the compliment graciously with a big smile.

Recognizing Rude Behavior

Whenever you are out in public, it's possible to notice the rude behavior of people being inconsiderate and disrespectful to each other: pushing past someone to get through a door, not saying thank-you after purchasing something, loud aggressive discussions or demanding service. Make a special family outing to collect data on rudeness. Whenever it is noticed that someone is being rude, point it out to the children and explain why it is rude behavior. Make sure you're not rude in noticing and pointing out the behavior. Write down the rude behavior you see on 3" x 5" index cards. When you get home, place the cards face down on a table. Pick a card. The person who wrote the card describes the details of the rude behavior they saw. Whoever wants to can play-act the roles of those involved in the incident, this time replacing the rude behavior with polite respect.

When Friends Come Over

When your children are at an early age, start talking about how one should act when friends come over to play, or when your child goes to play at someone else's house. When your child is as young as three, you can talk about how you will greet his friend at the door, then let the friend pick out the first thing to do. It is hard for kids to put their friends first, but that is the rule when someone is a guest in your home. Some other concepts to discuss might be: waiting to be invited, obeying the rules of the house, being helpful while you are at someone else's house, cooperating when choosing activities, playing with the child who invited you, not ignoring your guest if they don't want to do the same thing you do, asking before using anything that doesn't belong to you, putting away everything you take out, and thanking the host and their parents for allowing you to come over. Keep reaffirming the concept that adults like children who behave well, and will tend to invite back children who have good manners.

Thank-You Notes

Friends and family members will smile when they get a thank-you note from the child they have given a gift or a kindness to. It might be fun to have a basket of cards, envelopes, markers, and crayons conveniently available whenever someone wants to write. After a birthday party or holiday, schedule a time to sit with your child and help them. There are a few things to remember about thank-you notes, which should only be two to three sentences long: send them within a week of receiving the gift, mention what the gift was and why it was appreciated, and, if money was sent, write what might be bought with it. If your child is too young to write their own thank-you, let them dictate it and draw a picture. Computer generated cards are nice as long as they are personalized; handwritten cards seem to convey more of the child's own personality.

Who Would You Want to Live With?

Families that live together in a shared space usually have acceptable behaviors that everyone agrees upon: picking up after yourself, sweeping the floor if you track in dirt, putting the toilet seat down after use, putting the lid on the toothpaste, throwing away empty containers instead of putting them back into the refrigerator. Get everyone together and have fun writing a mock ad for the newspaper describing the person you would all like to have living in your house. Start like this: "Wanted, a housemate who..." When the letter is finished read it out loud.

WANTED: Fun Person who likes To Laugh.

Guests at Play

Having guests to your home for dinner is a fun way for children to practice their manners. A few days before the dinner occurs, have a practice run. Pick one or two family members to pretend to be dinner guests. Have a playful and instructional practice which demonstrates welcoming the arriving guest, taking the guest's jacket, hat, or purse, making introductions, sharing a refreshment and conversation before the meal, calling people to dinner, helping the guest get seated, serving the meal, practicing dinnertime manners and conversation, moving from the dinner table to after dinner conversation location, and finally, getting their jacket, hat, or purse upon departure. Make comments, and give ideas of ways to talk, and what to do, as you act out the manners involved in each of these parts of entertaining. When everyone has mastered the manners involved, have your dinner party!

Being a Good Sport

What better way to teach a child what good sportsmanship looks like than to let them see it in a fun way. In this game, the loser gets to choose between being a poor loser or a good sport. The fun part is acting it out. A poor loser would cheat, whine, foot stomp, cry foul-play, or threaten revenge. The good sport would follow the rules, acknowledge the winner's expertise, shake the winner's hand, and smile graciously, happy with their performance. The good sport would not celebrate too much when they win, nor complain loudly if they lose. They would never blame someone else for their loss. The players have a game of tic-tac-toe and those not playing watch the spectacle. The audience does their part by responding to the game with appropriate boos and hisses when poor sportsmanship is demonstrated, and with cheers, chants, and clapping when good sportsmanship shines through.

Community Building

Never underestimate the impact that can be made by one single person who cares. We must teach our children that they can and do make a difference. When they smile at someone who looks sad, feed someone who is hungry, or reach out to meet a new neighbor, they are adding goodness to the world. Each seed of goodness makes a big difference. The world we want to exist must be planted in the minds of our children.

"We must remember that one determined person can make a significant difference, and that a small group of determined people can change the course of history."
—Sonia Johnson

One Child, One Flower

The world we want to exist must be planted in the minds of our children. Flowers are beautiful and hopeful symbols of life. The next time you read about a tragic event in the world, such as a war that is going on, a school bus crashing, or a child dying of cancer, buy one flower for every life lost. Plant the flower at home, at school, or at a park, in memory of the loss. Talk to your children about how sad it is and have them imagine what it would be like if the tragic event happened in their community. Think about the children who died when you plant, care for, and look at the flowers. They may even want to write a poem, glue it to a stick and put it into the ground next to the flowers. Give them the feeling that no matter how big the world's problems are, their caring matters.

Volunteering

Caring for other people outside the family teaches children so much about compassion and empathy. It broadens a child's understanding of different types of people and different lifestyles. It creates a person who will go through life helping others. It gives the family a sense of purpose which creates closeness. There are many things that families can volunteer to do together. Talk together about the causes your family might be interested in, then call organizations in your area to see what is available. Here are a few ideas.

- Adopt a grandparent: an elderly neighbor or resident of a nearby nursing home may not have any family in the area.
- Adopt a family: find a poor family in your area to give food or clothes to once a month, or presents on a holiday or birthday.
- Adopt a handicapped or disabled person: include them on family outings or once a week for a family dinner.
- Books-to-go: see if your library would let you deliver books to homebound neighbors.
- Serve food at a homeless shelter.
- Write a letter to a legislator about an issue important to you as a family.
- Pick a public place to clean up or organize a neighborhood clean up.
- Visit a nursing home or hospital regularly.

Kids may be scared at first of some of the above ideas, but once they start meeting people, they will feel happy to be helping others.

Recycle

Part of caring for yourself and caring for others is caring about the earth. After all, it is our children's children who may have to live in a world that has no rainforest. Inform your children about environmental matters so they will care about the earth and want to do something to ensure its beauty and health. Kids are serious recyclers once they understand their role in being responsible for the earth. They love the sense of purpose behind flattening those boxes, bagging newspapers, crunching cans, and rinsing plastic. If recycling has not been part of your family until now, get organized and start. Your local garbage company may already pick up recyclables with the rest of your garbage once a week.

Read a Newspaper Together

Find and cut out an appropriate newspaper article to read together each day. There are often interesting articles on family life, world events, political arguments, fine arts, and people. This will create a personal interest in what is going on in the world, in other people's lives, and in learning new things. It will give your children the chance to ask you questions, and for you to ask them their opinions. If children are too young to read, you might just summarize the article for them in language they will understand. When your child is old enough to read the paper herself, assign her the job of picking the article for the family to read and discuss.

Pen Pals

Children often like the idea of communicating with children in different countries. It's interesting to find out what they do in school, what their families do together, what food they eat, etc. Making friends with children in another country also teaches your children how similar people are where thoughts, values, and emotions are concerned. Websites devoted to penpal topics:

www.epals.com
members.agirlsworld.com
www.world-pen-pals.com
www.pen-pal.com

Know Your Neighbors

Community building really starts with each person reaching out to one another. There are many ways to get your neighborhood together so that friendships can develop. Once together, it's also possible that you can help each other with things like child care, car pools, and emergency care. Here are a few ideas to get to know your neighborhood:

- Have a neighborhood block party. Put a flyer in each person's mailbox inviting them to the party. Everyone can bring a dish of food to eat. The party can be at someone's house, out in the street, or at a nearby park.
- Start an afterschool child care service. Find out which mothers are home after school on what days. If children are old enough to go home alone, but you are not at home, have them call a designated neighbor to make sure they made it home. Be creative and work together.
- Create a co-op program with special skills like plumbing, computer work, carpentry, or advertising. Instead of paying each other, you could trade hours. If not, at least you will know what each of your neighbors do for a living, and can give them your business.
- Start a neighborhood newsletter. One page is enough to start. Announce birthdays, deaths, births, etc. Kids could submit articles. This would be a good place to bring up things like traffic speed through the neighborhood, lawn mowers going before a certain time or an upcoming block party.

Part Four: Building Character

Courage

It takes great courage to be true to yourself, to go against popular opinion, or to stand up for a cause. It takes great courage to face a fear. Courage does not have to be a grand feat, it can be as simple as saying no. A child learns to be courageous by confronting and then working through the things they are afraid to do. When they learn to step forward to do something they believe in, even though the fear is still present, they will understand what courage feels like.

"The bravest thing you can do when you are not brave is to profess courage and act accordingly."
—Corra May White Harris

What Courage Is

Children might be confused as to what courage actually is. They may think it means fighting the bully, doing something one of their friends has dared them to do, or jumping off a cliff into water. Anytime someone calls them a wimp, scaredy cat or baby, they may think they should show their courage. Adults know that courage isn't like that at all. Courage is taking reasonable risks for a good cause, standing up for what you believe, standing up for the rights of others, and being who you are regardless of others' opinions. Tell your children stories of courageous people you know, and tell them about the times in your life you felt you had courage. Together, make a decorative card or book that describes what courage is. Whenever you see your child doing something courageous, make sure to notice it and tell them how much you admire their courage.

Badge of Courage

It takes courage for a child to remain true to themselves when friends are encouraging bad behavior. Take time together to design, construct, and decorate a badge of courage. It could be pin, pillowcase, banner, vase, or anything else to honor your child. As you're constructing the badge, talk about how easy it is to go along with the crowd and how difficult it is to go against it. Start when your children are young by praising them for being caring individuals. When you hear a story about a bully at school, or the weird kid in class, talk about how it would feel to be that child. Encourage your child to tell you when they feel they have acted with courage. Then, make a big deal about it by having a family ceremony to present the child with the homemade badge. They can keep the badge until someone else in the family does something courageous. At that time, let the former badge of courage holder conduct the next ceremony.

Act as if You Can

Part of being afraid of doing something or confronting someone is the feeling you just aren't capable of doing it. Help your children overcome their fear by teaching them how to visualize.

This is how to instruct your child in visualization technique:
Have your children sit down and close their eyes. Take the situation they are afraid of, and have them see themselves acting out the situation in their own mind. They need to see themselves going through all the

motions and words. Then, they have to see how they will deal with the outcome. Let them run through the scenario in their minds as many times as they want. If they are having a hard time visualizing, you may want to suggest a few visualizations in story form while they try to see the scene in their mind. After they have visualized it a few times, ask them what they thought about. Say together at least five times, "I can do this."

Face Your Fears

Children can be scared of many things: the dark, monsters, being alone, robbers, storms, etc. It's hard to be courageous when it's dark out and your mind wanders. Here are a few ideas of things to do which will encourage your child to be brave:

- Play in the dark. Give your child a big piece of paper, and have them draw things with all the lights off. You will be sitting in the room with them, turning on the lights after each drawing is complete. Laugh together as you look at the silly picture.
- Play tag in the dark. The rules have to be simple so that no one gets hurt. Move furniture to create a safe space. This is a slow tag where each person simply reaches their arms out trying to touch someone else.
- Turn off the lights and have your child touch objects you have gathered; then, have them guess what they are.
- Draw a picture of a friendly monster who will defend your child from the scary ones. It also helps to make a sign and put it on the door that says, "No monsters allowed!"
- When a storm comes to town, act it out. Howl like the wind, yell like the lightning, tap like the rain.

Night Time Sleep Out

Having the courage to get out and do something that you've never done before can be a little scary. A child cannot learn how to have courage if they never have a chance to confront a fear. Here's a chance to confront a few common fears, such as the dark, being outside all night, or being away from home, in a fun way. Spend a night together under the stars. No fancy camping equipment, just a blanket to put on the ground and a sleeping bag to crawl into. Listen to the night sounds, smell the night air, wish on the stars, and feel the joy of waking up covered with dew. Make a big deal of telling everyone how brave your child was while in the wild.

Truthing

The pathway towards trust is lined with handrails of truth. The only way to build trust is to be honest. There is no other way. Getting a family to function in this truthful space means that family members have to trust each other. Trust is built when the truth is told and love remains constant. When a family values honesty, each family member will be able to express the truth in their lives, trusting in the family's ability to support them.

"We arrive at truth, not by reason only,
but also by the heart."
—Blaise Pascal

Reward Honesty

How do you reward honesty when a child has told you the truth about something they have done wrong? Often, after encouraging children to be honest, a parent will then give the child a punishment of some sort. This usually makes the child feel that next time they should not tell the truth so they can avoid the punishment. The important thing is to teach children to take responsibility for their actions; that means that once they tell you the truth, have them come up with ways they can make up for what has been done. Reward any honest admission by saying something like this, "I'm so pleased you were able to tell me the truth. Think for a few minutes about something you can do to make the situation better."

Describe It Honestly

Kids are great at describing things with great embellishment: "that mean girl in class wrote all over my paper" (when she accidentally made a small pencil mark), "he ate the whole box of cereal for breakfast" (when he really ate the last bowl), "I'm the dumbest one in class" (when they didn't get the perfect score they wanted). Play this game, called Snap Shot to show kids the difference between describing something honestly, and embellishing it. Our minds take mental pictures all day long. Pretend your eyes are a camera. Look at something in your house, then blink. Each person describes their snap shot as honestly as they can; then they describe it with great embellishment. After you have talked about a snapshot of something in the house, ask each person if they can remember an incident that they saw at school or at work that day. From now on, when your child comes home with a story that seems a little embellished, you might ask her if that was an accurate snap shot.

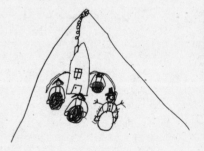

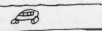

When a Child's Truth Is Embarrassing

Most parents will experience the embarrassment of a child's innocent question ("Why are you so fat?"), silent stare (at the person with green spiked hair), or spoken truth ("That man is ugly"). Children do these things naturally, and seem to be much more comfortable with, and curious about, the truth than adults are. They should not be made to feel bad about this. It is the child's way of observing the world and learning from it. Sit down and tell your children stories about things you did as a child that embarrassed your parents. Let them ask you questions about the stories, and see how honestly you can respond. Through this storytelling, discuss how the people about whom the comments were made might feel. End by saying that you want them to keep being honest about everything they are thinking, but that they need to be careful not to hurt someone's feelings by saying it loudly or in front of the person.

Making Judgments vs. Stating True Feelings

There is a difference between making a judgment about something, and expressing your feelings. When true feelings are expressed, one of the following phrases is usually used: I like, I don't like, I want (to), I don't want (to). A judgment is a statement that implies something is good or bad. "Dinner is terrible" is a judgment; "I don't like peas" is a true feeling. When people share their true feelings, they are able to feel closer to each other because their feelings express what's inside. When people make judgments, the closeness disappears because the judgment expresses something outside of the person. When we want to say something honestly, it's important to express it with feelings instead of a judgment. Get everyone together and play with this concept. Pick a subject to talk about: how the home looks inside or out, the last vacation, chores, etc. Starting your statements with "I like, I don't like, I want (to), I don't want (to)," everyone share their true feelings. After a while, switch the conversation to everyone making judgments. Talk about the two very different tones set by the two types of communications. From now on, make an effort to express feelings instead of judgments when communicating with each other.

The Ring of Truth

Being honest with yourself means opening your mind to the way you feel about certain things. When something rings true, it brings the feeling of "Aha!" Sometimes that "Aha!" might hurt a little, or make you feel you need to change your behavior, which is okay. Here's a game to play that will make clear what it means to hear the ring of truth. Get a bell and make up playing cards out of index cards. Write the following statements on each card:

- I don't spend enough time with my family.
- I feel ignored.
- I'm getting my needs met at home.
- I feel good about myself.
- I want to contribute more to my family.
- Sometimes I want to get away from everyone.
- These activities are not doing any good.
- I don't feel very important here.
- We don't spend enough time together.
- Nobody takes me seriously here.
- Our family gets better all the time.
- We should have company over more often.

Dream up any statements of your own to put on more cards. With the cards all face down, each person in turn pick up one card and read it out loud. Everyone pause to notice if they feel the "Aha!" ring of truth. Be sure the bell is placed within reach so that each person who feels the ring of truth within can pick up the bell to ring it. After the game is over, talk about how it made you feel to realize you had certain feelings you may not have been aware of before.

Bottle Your Judgments

Resentment usually begins with a judgment: "My sister is a pig, she always leaves the room a mess"; "Mom never lets me stay up like other kids"; "Dad doesn't care about us, all he does is play tennis." As long as the picture of family life includes judgments about family members as being "bad" or "wrong," then resentment occurs. Instead of proclaiming a judgment to the family member you are mad at, write it down on a piece of paper and put it into a bottle (everyone can use the same bottle). A bottle with a narrow neck works best since the judgments can't be taken out. Put the paper in the bottle with the intention of putting your judgment someplace while you have a chance to think about it. A truth will usually come to your mind in a few days that will allow you to see your judgment in a different way. If after a week you still feel the same about your judgment, talk in a caring way to the person the judgment is about.

What to Do with Secrets

Some secrets are fun to keep to yourself or to share with friends: a present for an upcoming birthday, a club's secret code word, or someone you like at school. But some secrets are kept with a feeling of fear, or to prevent negative consequences if the information is revealed, or to make someone feel left out. This is the kind of secret that causes family members to feel distant and out of touch. It is important to talk about these kind of secrets with someone. Get the family together and talk about good secrets and bad secrets. Let each person know that they are loved no matter what, and that family is a safe place to talk. Everyone try to think of a secret that they might want to keep because they are afraid to say it. If it's too difficult to say it out loud to everyone, write it down on a piece of paper for nobody to see. Getting it out of your head and into words is a good first step. Listen to the brave family members who are willing to reveal their secrets without making any judgments. This will make your house a safe place for family members to say secrets they were afraid to tell before.

True Feelings Being Heard

Can you say your true feelings without needing others to agree with you, support you, or take care of you? In other words, could it be enough just to be listened to? How would it be to say to another family member, "I want people to be nicer to me," and only have that person say, "I hear what you're telling me and I appreciate you saying your feelings." Get the family together and sit in a circle. Focus the discussion on how people in the family treat each other. One person starts by sharing a true feeling (I want, I don't want, I like, I don't like) with the person to their right. The one listening says, "I hear what you're telling me and I appreciate you saying your feelings." Then the listening person becomes the next to share a true feeling with the person on their right. Follow around the circle in this way three full times. How does it feel to be listened to?

Patience

Few are born patient. The desire for immediate gratification is one of a baby's first experiences. It takes a while but with encouragement most children do get better and better at waiting. Patience is like a deep breath that slows us down long enough to act wisely, it teaches us to wait and to be still. A patient mind learns to entertain itself while it waits, and a patient heart learns to listen until it understands. A child who learns patience has found a tool that will help greatly in overcoming the frustrations of life.

"Adopt the pace of nature:
her secret is patience."
—Ralph Waldo Emerson

Waiting with Patience

Children often get frustrated when they have to wait too long for something to happen. It's hard to wait patiently. Routine helps kids order their lives so they know what follows what in their daily schedule. That way, they don't get frustrated when their bed has to be made before they run outside to play, or they have to wait until after lunch to go to the library. Talk about your child's schedule. Write it down to help them see when they have free time and when they are doing chores or homework. If there is some event they are waiting for, put it on the calendar so they can see how long they will have to wait. If you have many children that all need the same computer or piano to practice, make a daily schedule. Whenever you see your child waiting patiently for a snack, a turn on the phone, or their computer time, make sure to acknowledge how patiently they are waiting.

Working Through a Task

When a child is doing a task and gets frustrated because they don't think they can complete it, don't jump in to save them immediately. Giving a child room to struggle teaches them how to be patient with themselves as they slowly figure the problem out. You may have to step in with positive words like, "You can do it, just close your eyes for a moment, then try again." If your child starts ripping something up, or throwing it on the ground, help them to start again by breaking the task down into smaller parts. Make sure your child has a reasonable chance to succeed at the task; if not, change the task into one he or she can succeed at.

Centerpiece

Remember "sharing time" in pre-school? Tonight, have each family member bring some small object that is important to them to the dinner table. Together, arrange an attractive centerpiece out of each person's item. Each person share the importance of the object they brought. Everyone listen patiently without interrupting or making comments. It takes patience to listen carefully.

When Angry, Seek Patience

The problem with anger is that it makes us want to respond immediately with fury. Kids have as hard a time controlling their anger as adults do; they feel like yelling at their siblings, hitting or biting each other, and getting even. So, the rule every parent needs to remember is to count to ten before they respond to anything when they are feeling angry. Better yet, say what you are doing in that ten second time so your child can hear you: "I'm feeling so angry, I will stop and think what I want to say." Repeat this a few times until you are calmer. Don't be surprised when your child does the same thing the next time he or she is angry.

Patience Project

The only way to learn patience is by practicing it. Set up things to do weekly that require patience: going outside and waiting for a bird to come eat a piece of bread, planting seeds that take time to grow, building something that will take a few days to complete, writing an ongoing story, fishing, bird watching, going on a walk and searching for a particular leaf, making bread and waiting for it to rise all day. Each time your child patiently waits for something that does come to pass, they grow used to the idea that many things in life take a while to happen.

Tolerance

Tolerance is an attitude of acceptance toward life and toward others that allows for different views, opinions, lifestyles, beliefs, practices, and actions. In every person's mind, there seems to be a set of expected standards or desires. When those standards aren't met, something has to be tolerated for a period of time. If we can learn to tolerate various interactions with life that may not be identical to our own standards, we learn to be open-minded, listening to others as we respect and understand them. Most of all, we can learn to tolerate our own shortcomings with a positive and accepting attitude.

"No life is so hard that you can't make it easier by the way you take it."
—Ellen Glasgow

Family Moods Are Contagious

When you live in a house shared with other people, you learn to tolerate all kinds of moods, both good and bad. You probably didn't know that moods, like colds, are contagious. As a family, investigate this idea. Next time you see a family member in a bad mood, see if you can identify the moment their mood affects you, and you start feeling bad. Say it out loud so everyone can hear, "I can feel your mood right now." Just noticing that this occurs may stop the mood from being passed on. This might be a good time to talk about "cold etiquette"; after all, you wouldn't sneeze right in someone's face. As a family, you could encourage the idea of taking a time out yourself if you are feeling in a bad mood. Talking is a good idea if you can, but if you are simply feeling lousy, go rest.

Stay Calm in Your Child's Storm

Staying calm when your child is angry, having a temper tantrum, calling you names, or misbehaving is a great way to teach your child how to get through their own emotional storms. Close your eyes for a brief second as the storm starts, then repeat to yourself, "I will stay calm, no matter what" (as many times as you need to). Then do the following, depending on the problem.

- Calmly state the consequence for the unacceptable behavior: "Go to your room until you can calm down" or "We don't call names in this house, so you will not be able to go to your friend's house today." Make sure there is some consequence that matches the child's behavior.
- When the child has calmed down, ask them to think of a better way of handling the situation next time.

When Things Are Beyond Our Control

So much time is wasted worrying about things that have already happened, things we cannot change, or things that are beyond our control. It's important that children learn from you how to tolerate mistakes in themselves and in others. It starts when a five-year-old tracks mud across the carpet. There are two ways to handle the situation: scream your anger, or calmly say that the damage is done and there is nothing that can magically make it "un-happen." The most important thing we can teach children about mistakes is that there are only two things you can do with a mistake: do the best you can to fix the problem, and learn from it so it doesn't happen again in the future. If you respond to your child with anger and accusations when they make a mistake, you can be sure your child will respond in the same way when she sees a mistake being made.

I Can't Stand It When...

A few times each day, parents usually hear the phrase, "I can't stand it when Suzy uses my paints," or "I can't stand the way Bill teases me all the time." Whenever you hear that phrase, ask the person the following: "What do you need to do so that you can stand it?" Talk through ways of solving the problem at hand, or ways of speaking in a kind tone about the person they "can't stand." The truth is, we can each tolerate quite a bit, and we do each day in family life. Point out the times your child said they couldn't stand something, and what they did to make it through. Don't solve the problem for your child; just encourage them to change the situation so that they can stand it.

Helpfulness

Daily burdens are made lighter when carried by two. Each day the list of things to be done to keep a household functioning is endless. The children have homework, lessons, and chores, while the adults work, upkeep the home, prepare meals, and attend to the children. If each person in the family has a helpful attitude—one that is on the lookout for ways they can help out—each person's burden will be much less. An attitude of helpfulness creates a feeling of togetherness within the family as everyone works toward common goals.

"After the verb 'to love,' 'to help' is the most beautiful verb in the world."
—Bertha Von Suttner

Make a Chore Chart

Rather than having to tell your children each day what chores you would like them to do, make a chart. The chart should have the days of the week across the top of the paper, and the chores to be done down the side. On each day, put the first initial of the person's name who will be doing that chore. This is a good way to make sure that chores are equally distributed; things that don't need to be done every day can be spread out throughout the week. It also puts the responsibility on the child to look at the chart and make sure they have done their jobs. You may want to have a check-off system at the end of each day to make sure all the chores were done.

Days	Brian	Nicole	Jake
Monday			
Tuesday			
Wednesday			
Thursday			
Friday			

Move Furniture

Sometimes furniture gets boring if it sits in the same place all the time, or maybe a shelf gets too cluttered, or a dried flower arrangement looks old. Get the family together and look around the living or family room and ask for suggestions of things to be moved or changed. Pick one that everyone feels comfortable with and change it together. When children participate in creating the home environment, they are more likely to take pride in it and be helpful in cleaning it up.

Help Wanted

A fun way to make children feel they are choosing their chores is to put up a "Help Wanted" bulletin board somewhere in your house. Write up advertisements for the jobs you need done: "Looking for someone strong to help me move some books," "If you have a green thumb, answer this ad for weed pulling, leaf raking, and seed planting." or "Window washer needed, apply inside." You can either write an amount to be paid for each job wanted ad, or, if you don't believe in paying children for chores, you could require them to answer a certain number of ads each week.

Cleaning Game

Pick a day for everyone to do chores together. You will be amazed how fast you can clean a house when you do one room at a time, with each person doing their part. Make it fun by hiding a few pieces of candy or surprises before you start. Every once in a while blow a whistle, ring a bell, or simply announce "treat time." Then, everyone can hunt for the treats and enjoy them together.

Getting Things Put Away

How often do you walk around your home stepping around things that have been left wherever they were last used? The goal is to get kids to be helpful whenever they notice a mess they've created. However, as they are learning this intuitive skill, you may need to give them consequences for not being helpful. The following is guaranteed to free your house of clutter in a short time. As you see things left around the house, collect them immediately and put them away somewhere. After a few days, have an auction. The person whom the object belongs to gets a chance to buy it back first. The objects must be bought back at the auction with things like time spent doing chores, helping their sibling, reading time, etc. If the person doesn't care enough about what is being auctioned to buy it back, someone else can.

Chores Can Be Fun

Pick a chore that all the children can participate in: clean up the play room, straighten up the family room, scrub the bath tub, pick up trash from the yard, organize books or newspapers. Make the chore fun by turning it into a game of tag. A parent needs to be the supervisor, giving each child two to three minutes of chore time while the rest of the children play nearby. When a child's time is up, the supervisor calls "Next!" and the child who has done a part of the work runs to tag the next child in order. Then this child runs to the chore area for their two minutes of work. Keep this going until the chore is done. You might even want to time how long it takes for the chore to be completed and keep a record sheet.

Responsibility

A responsible person can be counted on to do what is theirs to do. They can be depended on to do what they say, and can be left with a chore or assignment with the knowledge that they will do their best. Responsibility is a trait that is learned as tiny steps are taken. Children get to be more responsible as they become capable of new and challenging tasks. As they succeed in taking on responsibilities, children grow more confident in their abilities. Once a child has tasted the positive response to his being responsible, he is more motivated to be in charge of his own actions.

"Parents can only give good advice or put them on the right paths, but the final forming of a person's character lies in their own hands."
—Anne Frank

What Responsibility Means

When children can set goals and then use their own problem-solving skills to achieve those goals, they are learning responsibility. Chores can teach children how to be responsible both around the house and with personal care as early as two years old. It's important that the job be appropriate for the age, and that parents take time to teach their child how to do the job. Here are a few job ideas:

- 2–3 years: brush teeth, turn out lights when they leave the room, pick up toys.
- 4 years: wash and dry hands, dress themselves, take toys out of the bathtub, feed a pet, get the newspaper.
- 5–6 years: make their bed, get mail, water plants, pick up their own clothes and put them away, carry dishes to and from the table, empty the trash.
- 7–9: organize their own homework and clothes, weed garden, care for a pet, clean the bathroom, wash and shampoo themselves, make their own lunch, dust, vacuum.
- 10–12: simple cooking, mow lawn, help with grocery shopping, care for younger siblings, organize their own drawers and closet, do their own laundry.

Let kids participate in the planning of which jobs get done and when they get done. Once a schedule has been agreed upon, stick to it. It's easier for your child to be responsible if the job is defined and expected.

What's Yours?

Members of your family are each responsible for what is theirs. Things that belong only to them might be shoes, bed, lunch box, toothbrush, personal supplies, or homework. Things that belong to the whole family might be a car, television, stereo, furniture, or a trampoline. Sit around the table, letting each person mention one thing that belongs only to them, and how they take care of it. Keep going around the circle, taking turns until each person says everything they can think of. After individual items are talked about, go around the circle and say all the things that belong to the family. Then ask, "How does each person take care of group items?" This exercise may help everyone see that it takes cooperation from all members to be responsible for the things that belong to the family.

You Can Count on Me

When family members can count on each other to take responsibility for certain things, everyone benefits. Sometime when everyone is together, go around and have each person finish the sentence, "You can count on me... (to pick you up from school, for emotional support, to do my chores, to feed the pet, to buy groceries, to play with you, for free advice, to brush my teeth, to trim the lawn)." Keep going around with each person saying one thing each time, until there is nothing left to be said. Everyone take a few moments to think of a new responsibility they would be willing to take on and finish the sentence, "My new one is going to be that you can count on me to/for..."

Working Together

Pick a group project to do together: washing the car, cleaning out the garage, planting a garden, cleaning the house, etc. Plan together how the project will be completed. Each person will have to take on certain responsibilities in order for the project to succeed. Here's what you will need:

- a list of what needs to be done
- the order the work needs to be done in
- who will do what
- assignment of supervision (if needed)
- getting supplies together

Everyone in the family will be amazed at how much can be done, and how much fun it is when everyone works together. Shared responsibility makes everyone's job easier.

Understanding a Parent's Responsibility

Parents are responsible for many things in the home that children never notice. Take an hour or so one evening, and lift all parental responsibility and authority. For the parent, this means simply being there; not teaching discipline or manners, not giving directions, not taking control of things, not being the one with the answers. For the children, this means doing things on their own; not asking for help with chores, homework, or projects, not asking for a referee with disagreements, or to be fed, or to have their problem solved, or for a decision. After the hour is over, talk about how it felt to each of you. Did you like it? Do the kids feel like they could take responsibility for more things themselves without being told? Who was it most difficult for, and why?

New Responsibilities

Children need to be taught new responsibilities when they are ready and able to achieve them; a two year old may not be able to make her bed and dress herself, but a ten year old should be expected to. Observe your child for a day, noticing what they are responsible for, and how well they accomplish their set tasks. For each of your children, think of one new responsibility they are ready to learn, or an old responsibility that is not being done consistently. Be willing to commit a little time each day to helping your child with the behavior until it becomes a habit. Discuss the new responsibility with your child. Then be there to help them for a little while until they learn it. When your child starts doing the behavior without your help or suggestion, give them praise, praise, praise.

Most Responsible Thing to Do

Get some 4" x 6" cards, and write each of the following situations on a card:

- I forgot to take my lunch.
- I lost my house key.
- The toilet overflows.
- I get home and no one is there.
- I fall and cut myself.
- I need a ride and someone I don't know offers to take me.
- A friend does something bad and I know about it.
- I break mom's favorite vase when she's not home.
- I owe a friend money but don't have any to pay it back.
- It's a family occasion but I want to go out with a friend.
- My sister/brother lends me a sweater and it gets torn.
- The house next door is burning and the fire truck arrives.
- I hear my mom say something on the phone that worries me.

Make up some of your own too.

To play the game, put all cards face down in the middle of the table. The first person picks up a card and reads it. Everyone playing gets to think what the most responsible thing to do would be in that situation. The person with the card gets to call on each person and listen to their opinions. After all the opinions have been given, using bits and pieces of any of the opinions offered, the cardholder announces their version of the most responsible action. In the same way, the cardholder listens to all opinions about what the least responsible thing to do would be. Each person gets to be cardholder until all the cards are gone.

Safety First

Take some time to talk about safety issues in your home: what to do in case of fire, how to react if someone is hurt, who to call in case of an emergency. Make a family plan to deal with each one of these things: have a fire drill, take a first aid class or buy a book and go over the procedures together, make a list of emergency numbers and place it by the phone and so on. Make a list of dangerous things to be fixed in your home: the missing light by the dark corner of the house, a broken window or chair, a rug that needs to be secured, cleaning supplies that are too reachable by children. It may take a few months to get to all of the above issues, but what a great way to learn responsible action!

If It's Your Mess...

One important responsibility each family member has is to clean up after themselves. Cleaning up the mess is never done because life goes on each moment: toys get brought out, towels are used, dishes are dirty, clothes need to be hung up, etc. Without anyone knowing this moment is coming, say, "Everyone stop and come here for a moment; we are going to walk through the house together!" As you walk through the house, point out everything that was left a mess: clothes on the floor, glasses left on the counter, beds not made, homework left on tables, washcloths on the floor, shoes next to the TV. Take as much time as needed to clean up the mess. Hopefully, everyone will get the message!

Irresponsibility Has Consequences

Natural consequences do occur when a child is irresponsible: homework can't be done if it's left at school, the child is too embarrassed to have a friend over if their room is a mess, the child is cold at school if a coat is left at home. Parents often feel it is their responsibility to save a child who has forgotten to bring or do something. We write excuses for homework not done, run back to the house to find that coat, or leave work to bring a lunch to school. It's hard to let your child experience the consequences of their behavior. However, if you have a child that is consistently irresponsible, and you keep rescuing them, they will not see their irresponsibility as a problem. Tell your child the new plan; that you will not be stepping in when he is irresponsible, then stick to it. It may be hard to see them experience the consequences, but you will be teaching them a lesson in real life.

Discipline

Discipline is a form of life training that, once experienced and when practiced, develops an individual's ability to control themselves. It allows us to devote ourselves to a task or goal until the task is complete. Discipline teaches us how to follow the rules that society and individual families have set up. Discipline from without generates discipline from within. The best form of discipline is the kind that comes from within, based on our developed sense of right or wrong and our own heartfelt goals. Discipline is a skill we continue to learn as we grow older and experience more challenging tasks.

"Some people regard discipline as a chore.
For me, it is a kind of order that sets me free to fly."
—Julie Andrews

Remembering Your Most Important Teacher

You are the most important teacher your child will ever have. Think back over the years to all the teachers you've ever had. Who stands out in your mind as the best, and why? Think about the tone in their voice, their patience in repeating instructions, their support, their willingness to let you make mistakes, their taking time to listen, their excitement and love of learning, their belief that their teaching was important, their belief in your abilities. Take ten minutes, close your eyes, and try to see the person in your mind as you remember what you felt in the presence of this teacher. Use this teacher as a model as you adjust your teaching style.

Taking a Simple Approach

The most important and simplest response you can make when you've got a "discipline problem" is to take the time to listen. Understanding the problem from the child's point of view is the first step. Think of a discipline problem you have right now with one of your children. Make an appointment with them to discuss this problem. See what happens when you approach the problem this way:

Honey, you know I have a problem with your _____. I really want to understand what's behind it, and I want to listen to everything you have to say about it. I will listen with an open heart and not speak until you are finished telling me your side.

When you approach your child with the single goal of understanding, you let go of the "who's right and who's wrong" battle. Your discipline problems with your children will diminish as they grow accustomed to being seen and heard.

Reinforcing the Positive

Think about how many times a day children are told they are doing something wrong: you didn't make your bed, stop hitting your sister, listen when I say something, I told you not to have a snack. Unfortunately, focusing on negative behavior does not produce positive behavior. Why not try this simple exercise for a day and see what happens? Completely ignore the things the children do wrong—pay no attention to them at all. Then, say something positive about anything and everything they do well: thanks for brushing your teeth without being reminded, you look nice, that was kind of you, great job putting your toys away, you solved that math problem well. Be as specific as you can when you praise something, so the child knows exactly what you like about their behavior. Your child just might begin to look for good things to do so they can get your praise and begin eliminating the negative behaviors they used to exhibit.

Sharing the Wisdom of Rules

Sometimes children think their parents make up the strangest rules. The following activity might shed light on why parents make up the rules they do. OK, Mom and Dad, sit down with the children and tell them the rules you had to follow when you were the same age as the children are now. Then, share your childhood feelings about the rules and whether you thought they were appropriate for you at that age. Now, share with the children whether or not you believe following the rules was a valuable experience. It might also be fun to tell the kids what happened if you didn't follow the rules!

Stop, Sit, and Breathe

If you have more than one child, there will be times when you think you might lose your mind "because of the children." They might be throwing things, screaming, yelling, arguing about chores, etc. Instead of you joining in with their screaming, here's an alternative. Go to where the children and the commotion are and have everyone stop, sit on the floor, and take three deep breaths. After the breaths, talking may resume in a soft manner. This will slow everyone down for a few minutes, and at the same time teach them a tool they can use on their own.

Growing a Habit

It takes self-discipline to acquire good habits. It also takes practice and lots of mistakes. Have everyone in the family decide on one personal habit they would like to improve: calling when they will be late, telling the truth, getting up earlier in the morning, being more cooperative, smiling more, saying please and thank you, exercising regularly. As a reminder of the habit you are working on, each person plant a bulb in the windowsill garden, or outside. Give yourself as long as the bulb takes to bloom to work on the habit. When each person's bulb begins to bloom, they can report to the family whether or not the habit has bloomed in them. Practice patience with each other and encourage the growth of each family member's new good habits.

"Bleep"

Pick a word or phrase that your family agrees they do not want in your home anymore, such as hate, stupid, shut up, sucks, or get out. Whenever the word or phrase is spoken, someone can earn a point by saying "bleep" to the person who said the phrase. Make a simple scoreboard to keep track of the points. As usual, the one with the most points is winning. At the end of each week, the winner gets the "bleep" award, whatever the family decides it is.

Choosing a Style of Disciplining

There are two sides to the coin of discipline. Anytime you have to discipline a child, there's what you do without thinking or under pressure, and then there's what you might do if you thought about it. Take a look at the two circles below and the words contained within them. Which circle do you mostly discipline from? Which circle do you wish to discipline from? As a reminder, cut a circle out of cardboard and write the words from each circle on it. Carry it around in your pocket like a coin. Whenever a situation arises that calls for discipline, consider taking out your discipline coin to remind yourself what you are working toward.

In the Land of Crime and Punishment

Have a group storytelling about a land where everyone has to be perfect. One person starts the story and each person adds a bit until the story is over. Start like this:

Once upon a time, there was a faraway land where nobody ever got away with anything. Whether the little boy forgot to brush his teeth, or the girl left her lunch box at school, or the teenager was late for curfew, or mom changed her mind, or dad left a mess in the kitchen; every little thing was noticed and punished. This was the Land of Crime and Punishment, where you weren't allowed to make mistakes or forget something, you couldn't be wrong about anything, you weren't supposed to change your mind, and nobody was ever forgiven because you were supposed to be perfect...

After the storytelling, talk about how everyone makes mistakes and that in a family everyone has to be understanding of circumstances and not seek to punish every imperfection.

Make Consequences Work

Figuring out consequences of misbehavior may take time, thought, and self-discipline, but this practice provides the child with a predictable, lifelike experience of the way things are. Real life misbehavior (not paying the phone bill) results in natural consequences (phone service is disconnected). Using a consequence instead of a punishment always produces more positive results. Begin with the list below and add to it any behaviors you have in your family that you think aren't acceptable. Think about logical or natural consequences that you could put into effect immediately. See if discipline becomes any easier under this system.

misbehavior	logical consequences	natural consequences
messy room	some things are taken away	they live in the mess
hits sibling	the hitter is removed until cooled down	sibling hits back
misses the school bus	child does extra chores for the amount of time it took parent to drive them	walks to school, arrives late

Why Bribery Doesn't Work

Bribing a child with money, candy, or outings teaches them manipulation. It also shows them that you are willing to negotiate, which will start them saying things like, "What will you give me if I do...?" It is easier at times to bribe a child, since the results are immediate and it's much easier than having to discipline them for not doing what you asked. But in the long run, you will lose your voice; your words won't be enough incentive. The other side of a bribe is a threat: "Do this or you'll be sorry!" With bribes and threats, the kids have you negotiating with them. Instead, give them certain tasks and rules that are non-negotiable; then, be consistent with the consequences for breaking the rules. The best way to motivate kids is by giving them words of appreciation or praise.

Behavior and Consequence Chart

Are you looking for a solution to the discipline problems in your house? Make discipline everyone's responsibility by making a behavior and consequence chart together. Get your family to decide on the behaviors that all of you do not want occurring in your house: hitting, yelling, calling names, talking back, rooms left messy, personal belongings left around the house. Decide what would be appropriate consequences if the behaviors occur. Make a chart putting behaviors in one column and consequences in a column next to the behaviors. Next time a behavior occurs, go to the chart, and calmly read off the consequence. Since everyone made the chart together, and agreed on the consequences for unwanted behavior, there is shared responsibility for the action taken.

Give Spontaneous Awards

Spontaneous rewards occur when your child has already done a good deed without being asked to do it: "You cleaned your whole room without my asking, so I want to take you on a bike ride." These are unlike bribes since the child did the behavior without expecting anything good to happen. The concept is that you look for good behavior and reward it by praise or some spontaneous reward. If you get in the habit of looking for the good behavior and rewarding it, instead of looking for bad behavior, you are giving your attention to a better cause. Every good behavior might not get a big reward, but a simple positive word will do. Today, be on the lookout for some good behavior the child does without being reminded; then, think of a spontaneous reward to give them. You will be amazed how your child will respond by performing more and more unsolicited good deeds.

Forgiveness

Forgiveness is both attitude and action. It's not always easy to forgive some-one when we have been hurt, and it's not easy to ask someone to forgive us when we have caused hurt. A forgiving attitude means understanding and accepting that human beings fall short of perfection in many ways. We have all done things we wish we could take back, do differently, or handle with more kindness. Forgiving action means that we have to actually do the for-giving or ask for the forgiveness.

"Forgiveness is an act of the will, and the will can func-tion regardless of the temperature of the heart."
—Corrie Ten Boom

Say You're Sorry

Whenever a child or an adult has done something to hurt someone else, they need to say they are sorry. Maybe it's as simple as losing your temper, or calling someone a name, or eating the last cookie someone was saving. The sooner an apology can be made, the better. When children are mad at each other it might be a forced "I'm sorry" as they growl at each other. The important thing is to get into the habit of approaching the other person after the hurtful event to make amends. Adults can set great examples by using the words "I'm sorry" with their child when they have done something wrong: "I'm sorry I was late picking you up," "I'm sorry I yelled at you." If hurtful names have been called, try this: the person who called someone a name has to say they are sorry first, then think of three nice things to say about that person.

Telling Your Fantasies about Life

Wherever family life falls short of being perfect is where forgiveness needs to happen. There would be nothing to forgive if frustration, anger, or hurt never happened. Have a storytelling session about this kind of a world. Start like this: "Once upon a time there was a man/woman/boy/girl named _____ and this is what her/his life was like...Each day they liked to...They had friends who...At night after work or school they..." The story includes descriptions of how they were treated, what they did and didn't have to do, what they had, where they went, what people did for them. Let each person tell their own story that reflects the kind of life they would like to have while living in a family.

Fessing Up to Shortcomings

No one can do everything right all the time. Every person has shortcomings, things about them that are not perfect. At dinner tonight, encourage each person to talk about one of the shortcomings they noticed in themselves today (lost patience, said or did something hurtful, too busy with self to think of others, forgot something). Children need to see that adults make mistakes too, and adults need to see that children do realize their errors. The most important thing to talk about here is that in the family, we all have to live with a certain amount of forgiveness and acceptance toward each person every day. We accept who they are and love them anyway.

Healing Rocks

When the way things are in your life does not match the way you want things to be, feelings of disappointment, hurt, and being let down are usually felt. Sometimes the only way to deal with these feelings is to express them, to accept them, and to surround the pain with forgiveness. Everyone needs to find a stone and bring it to a group gathering. Let each stone represent some recent event that brought disappointment or hurt feelings. Find a pretty glass container to put all the stones into. Each person can share what happened to them before they place the stone into the container. The stone is placed into the container with the complete willingness that the event, the feelings, and the person all be forgiven. Leave the container out where all can see, and encourage family members to add to it with new stones when new disappointing situations arise. Let the stones symbolize the healing that takes place when we share our feelings with one another.

About Holding a Grudge

A grudge is a feeling of resentment, bitterness, or ill will towards someone. It usually happens because someone or something has hurt our feelings. Sometimes it hurts so much that we cannot let go of the grudge; we want to hold it tight because it makes us feel better. Pick one of the family's uglier stuffed animals to be the designated GRUDGIE. Sit together in a circle and pass GRUDGIE around, letting each person hold it tightly as they describe a grudge they are holding, their reason for holding it, and their right to hold it. After everyone has a chance to talk, discuss how two people's relationship is affected when someone is holding a grudge. Maybe it can become a family tradition to give someone GRUDGIE whenever a grudge is being held against them. At least then the person would know about the grudge and could talk about it.

Releasing Guilt

Guilt is feeling bad about something because you think it is your fault. And since guilt that is held inside keeps people from feeling good, here's a way to let go of the guilt and reach forgiveness. Using a stack of 3" x 5" cards, have each person begin writing one item per card: "I'm sorry that I..., I feel guilty about it because..." After everyone has finished writing their cards, read them out loud (if everyone agrees). Everyone listens without making any comments. An alternative to reading them out loud is to read them silently to yourself. After the reading, have each person rip up their cards as they consciously let go of the guilt.

213

Taking Steps Toward Acceptance

How accepting are the adults in your family about people's differences? Family life is training for life in the world, and if we aren't able to accept individual differences among our family, how could we ever expect to do it in the world? So it seems that whatever steps are taken toward accepting differences in the family are steps toward world peace! Everyone think hard about someone who is very different from them. Go around and discuss those differences. Are any of the differences difficult to accept? Why? What are the similarities? What can each of you do to let this person see your acceptance of them?

Pin the Blame on the Donkey

Here's a game the whole family can play to have fun getting over pinning the blame on other people. Buy a donkey party game or simply draw a donkey and hang it on the wall. Each person gets a tail that represents the situation or person they feel like blaming for something. Everyone gets blindfolded and spun around three times; then, they try to pin the blame on the donkey. If the kids don't know what blame sounds like, remind them: I didn't do it she did, it was my teacher's fault for not giving me the page number, you never told me to do it, if you were on time I would have won, he lost it, she ate it, etc. Use this game as a humorous way to point out how much blame actually takes place. After playing this once, whenever you hear someone blaming someone else in the family, just say "hee haw."

Grudge Dump

A grudge dump is a place to throw away bad feelings. It can bring peace and forgiving habits to a family. Buy a small trash container and place it someplace where everyone knows what it is for. Next to it put some scraps of paper and pencils. Before each person goes to bed at night they write on the slip of paper the name of anyone they might be holding a bad feeling or grudge toward: maybe a sibling got to stay up later than was fair, someone got to sit in the front seat, someone's favorite meal was cooked again, someone got good grades and someone else did not, all the beds were left unmade again, or a teacher or friend said something mean. Once the name is written on the paper, scrunch it up in a ball or rip it to pieces and throw it away. If it is a situation where you have been hurt and need to talk to the person, simply hand your paper to that person and say "can we talk?"

Apology Letter

Sometimes it seems too hard to apologize to someone in person or over the phone. This is the time to write an apology letter. An apology letter could include the following: saying you're sorry for the mistake that was made, explaining what you could have done differently so that the mistake would not have occurred, and thinking of something you could do to mend the situation. End the letter by saying that you care about the person and don't want there to be any hard feelings between you. Encourage your children to take care of any hurt they might have caused right away so they don't have to worry about it.

Part Five: Challenges

Times of Trouble

There is nothing as valuable as family support when troubles arise in life. Family is a natural place to get encouragement, love, and understanding. It needs to be the place we feel most comfortable turning to for help and ideas. Often, as we share the trouble the problem gets lighter as feelings and fears are expressed. Making family a place where troubles are a normal part of life experiences gives everyone a sense of being able to work through whatever trouble arises without causing personal panic.

"There are two ways of meeting difficulties. You alter the difficulties or you alter yourself to meet them."
—Phyliss Bottome

Make a Timeline

The closer we are to a problem, the bigger it seems. If you can place your current problem within the context of your family's entire life, you might see how problems come and go. Once you remember that "huge" problem of two years ago and how it was resolved, the family might relax a little more, knowing that the current problem will also be resolved. Make a family timeline by taping several sheets of paper end to end. Draw a line though the middle of the entire length. At the left end, make a short vertical line through the timeline and date it with the year the family started. Mark each twelve-inch interval along the timeline with a vertical line, each one dated one year later. Take it one year at a time with everyone contributing everything they can remember, both the good and the bad. Write it down on the timeline. Keep working on this until you reach the current date and the current problem. Hang it up as a reminder of what your family has already accomplished.

Troubled Faces

In times of trouble, it's important to remember that laughter heals. It's also important to acknowledge that the troubled feelings do exist. Here is a fun way to laugh, and at the same time acknowledge that the troubled feelings are real. Think about how your face looks when you're feeling troubled. Sitting around in a circle, one person starts by dramatically putting on their troubled face and showing that face to the person next to them. That person imitates the shown face and turns to the person next to them to pass it on. The face gets sent all the way back to its owner. Each person gets a chance to send their troubled face around. It's OK to have a good laugh, especially when life is difficult.

Your Family and Mine

When there is trouble in your life, it sometimes helps to focus your sights on something positive that the family can all do together. Get your family together and plan a picnic at a nearby park. Invite your neighbors by putting a flyer in each of their mailboxes with a date, time, and directions to the park where the picnic will be held. When the day arrives, make sure to bring a few balls, a Frisbee, an extra blanket or two, name tags, a jug of water or lemonade, bandages, and a notebook so everyone can write their name, address, phone, and the ages of their children. Having and making new friends in your community gives the family people to reach out to in times of trouble.

Solve It Together

Sometimes trouble comes in the form of a problem within the family that hasn't been solved. Pick a current family problem: people missing mealtimes, someone moving in or out, a household environment issue or sharing housework. Announce the problem at hand and then let each person come up with as many ideas as they can about the way the problem could be solved. You may even want to write these ideas down. Once everyone has a chance to express their opinion, go around and let everyone say which solution they think is the best one. Discuss the solutions until everyone can agree on one solution that they would be willing to try. Try it; if it works, celebrate, if not, go back to your original list of solutions and try another one.

Rose

No life can contain only good and happy moments. A rose is a perfect symbol of beauty, grace, peace, and goodness. Its thorns are a perfect symbol of pain, adversity, and struggle. So many things in life contain both: the meal was perfect before the milk spilled, the new home was just right until the roof leaked, the bike ride was thrilling until the fall. The rose is a reminder to the family that both positive and negative things are part of daily life. Bring home a rose tonight to have a rose celebration. Let children hear their parents accepting the fact that things are good and bad: I am sad to get transferred but at least we'll get to see Paris; the bird died, but I have great memories of him; I failed a test, but I will do better next time. As everyone looks at the rose in the center of the table, share what happened. This can be done again whenever the need arises.

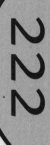

How Full Is Your Well?

When your inner well is full, you feel raring to go and on top of the world. But, when your inner well is empty, you feel out of steam. It's important to know how you're feeling because it affects how you act each day. Sit around the table with a pitcher of water and a transparent glass for each family member. One person at a time pours water into their glass to the level that matches how they are feeling, how full their well is. As you do this, talk about the reason the water level is at the place it is. Once you have done this, it will be easy to tell each other on a bad day that your well is empty. It also helps to know if someone's well is empty, since you might be able to help them find a way to fill it up by giving them a few minutes of peace, watching a younger sibling for a while, or giving a helping hand.

Stew On It Together

One thing we do when there are troubles on our mind is to stew about them; that means thinking constantly about them. When the family is having a hard time, why not stew on the problem together? Agree on one family problem for everyone to stew over. Each person pick a favorite vegetable to prepare for the stew you will make together for dinner. As each vegetable is added to the stew, give a little thought to the problem. As the hours go by, stir the pot any time you find yourself stewing about the problem. Enjoy the aroma floating throughout your home. During the meal, share with each other what you thought about during the day as you stewed.

Do What You Can

No matter what the problem, there are always things you can do to feel better, and there are always things that you wish you could do, but that, in reality, may be very difficult to achieve. It helps to do what you can whenever possible and to accept what you can't do. What happens when you don't know the difference? Here's a game to play to help everyone define problems and what can and can't be done about them. On pieces of paper or index cards, write down all the problems you can think of. Put all the cards face down on the table. Pick a card off the table and read the problem. Each person gets to say one thing they could do about the problem and one thing they couldn't do. Pick a new problem and continue in the same way until all the cards are picked.

Problem	Can do	Can't do
The weather is too cold	Wear sweaters	Make it warmer
Bully at school picks on me	Loudly say how I feel	Make the bully stop
Daily bus ride takes too long	Entertain myself on the ride	Make it go faster

Emotional First Aid Box

How quickly we run for a bandage if we've cut our finger. For most of us, it's hard to yell for help if we have been emotionally hurt. But every family can have an emotional first aid box. As a group, get or cut a bunch of blank cards about 2" x 3". On each card, you'll write one action that would make you feel better if you were hurting. Here are some starters:

- being listened to
- getting attention
- getting a hug
- being acknowledged
- taking a walk
- watching a movie
- listening to music

- watching the clouds
- having a reward
- being surprised
- eating a favorite treat
- calling a friend
- looking through a photo album
- being out in nature

Make up ideas of your own, then place them all in a small box. Decorate the box and the bandages if you want. Whenever you are feeling emotionally hurt, hand the box to someone in your family and get the help you need.

Trouble Pals

Think of a person in your life whom you feel comfortable telling your troubles. Maybe it's a family member, a friend, a co-worker, a teacher, or a neighbor. Ask them if they want to be your Trouble Pal. Whatever you tell your Trouble Pal has to be kept a secret. This is how Trouble Pals work. Whenever you are troubled, ask your pal, "Do you have a moment to listen to my trouble?" Tell your pal your trouble. Say all the things you would like to do about it, and what you feel you can't do anything about. Your Trouble Pal listens to you, and can even give ideas if you want them to. The most important thing to do if you have a trouble is to talk it out; then it won't seem so bad, and you may even talk your way into a solution.

Think about Someone Else

In times of trouble, we tend to get wrapped up in ourselves and our problems. It's all we think about, and it affects every aspect of our lives. Sometimes it helps to see the problems other people have, and try to do something to help them. In helping them, we feel stronger, happier, and more able to deal with our own problems, which sometimes don't seem like big problems anymore after looking at someone else's problems. Sit down together as a family and think about other people that might need your help: a family friend who just found out he has cancer, a homeless person, a family whose house just burned down. Talk about the possible ways of reaching out. Decide on a plan of action and do it soon; you will all feel better.

Shake Dance

Get the family together and reflect on the most recent experience each of you had that made you feel really upset. Think about who was involved, where it happened, what was said, and any other details that occur to you. When everyone has done this, you are ready to shake dance. The youngest child gets the action started by saying, "ready, get set, go!" Everyone leaps to their feet and lets all parts of their body shake and jiggle, releasing all the tension from the bad experience. Shake for at least five minutes, then sit down, relaxing from the exhilaration.

Grandest Teacher of All

Nature can teach us so much about rebuilding; plants die and new shoots begin to grow, the leaves fall and bud again in spring, a fire burns the forest to the ground but seedlings still grow, and on and on. When the family is going through hard times, go out into nature and talk about strength—the strength to start something again and let it grow. Talk about flexibility, the ability to sway and bend as the wind of trouble blows hard. Talk about the seasons that change just like feelings. There is peace to be gained by looking into the hand that holds us all, knowing that growth and change create life. In times of trouble, a positive attitude and outlook is the best tool we can give our children.

Create a Rainbow of Hope

There's a certain feeling of hope when a storm breaks and you see a rainbow appear. It's just one way Mother Nature has of constantly providing us with a glimpse at the mystery of life. Bring this symbol of hope down from the sky and right into your home. Get as large a piece of paper as you can find to make a rainbow on. The colors of crayons you need, starting in order at the bottom, are yellow, orange, red, green, blue, and purple. While you're working together, think about all of your hopes. When the rainbow is done, write all that you hope for across the rainbow: your hopes for yourself, your family, your friends, your community, your world.

When Kids Feel Stress

Kids do feel stress. It's impossible to make it disappear, but it is possible to give your child the tools to handle it. A parent's attitude and outlook on life can be the child's greatest tool. How do you handle stressful situations? If all the lights just went out because of an earthquake, would you express with delight that it's a perfect night to take your flashlight and go for a moon walk, or would you tense up, talking about every possible tragic thing that could happen? When driving your child to school in traffic, do you sit back and enjoy the time together, or do you drive bumper to bumper, condemning everyone else for driving poorly? Your child will pick up on your attitude, so take some time today to examine what you are communicating with your actions. The second tool you can give them is to love, accept, and respect them in whatever situation. That helps them to believe in themselves and to know that they are the same person no matter what happens. The third tool is to teach them to take ten deep breaths as soon as they feel the stress. A good way to teach relaxation is by pointing it out when you do it yourself. For example, "I feel so much stress today, I'm going to take ten deep breaths; then, I'm going outside with a cup of tea to look at something beautiful."

About Death

Children who are exposed to the idea of death as part of the life process are not so afraid of the concept as those who never talk about it. Most of us don't jump into discussing death with eager anticipation. However, if a space is made in family life to talk about loss, what it feels like, and what it means, the children will see it as a natural part of the life process. Children already have some concept in their own mind of what death is, so if facts are given it leaves less space for their imagination to make up scary thoughts. If children feel comfortable talking about death, they will be less afraid and have more understanding when someone close to them dies.

"The only truly dead are those who
have been forgotten."
—Jewish Saying

Exploring the Mystery of Life and Death

So many questions about life and death are unanswerable. Since people who are trying to answer the questions have not died yet, all answers are opinions, impressions, ideas, or beliefs. However, that is no reason to avoid discussing the topic. Start a mystery question box. Use any container with a lid. Cut a hole in the top so pieces of paper with questions written on them can be stored inside. Sit together and come up with every imaginable question about life and death: What makes us breathe? Why don't we remember being born? Why do I cry tears when I'm sad? Why do people die? Will I remember my life after I die? Will we see people we know when we die? Where will I go when I die? Put all the questions into the box and pick one out to discuss. Remember, all thoughts on the question are valid since the answers are unknown. Keep the box handy for future dinnertime discussions, and encourage everyone to add new questions.

Talking about Who Has Passed on

Many times death is not discussed in the family until someone dies. Yet by a certain age, children do understand that each of us will die. The more comfortable everyone can get discussing their fears and feelings about death, the more prepared and peaceful all will feel. Children may not know anyone who has died, but most are very curious and will ask many questions if given the chance. Take time to talk about somebody in your life who has died; how they died, when they died, what happened after they died, what the funeral was like, how you felt about it, if you still think of them, etc. Let the children ask all the questions they want and answer them as truthfully as possible.

Say It Today

Sometimes it feels safer to keep feelings to ourselves. However, expressing your feelings often to those you care about is important. If something would ever happen to them, you would at least know they were aware of how you felt, and that there was nothing left unsaid. Get everyone together to do a little letter writing. Write brief notes to all the people you care about; tell them how much you love them, forgive them for any hurt they have caused, tell them if there is something on your mind, etc. Write to the family members sitting around you as well as those at a distance. Get these messages delivered right away; you'll feel good about it.

Interviews with an Elder

Is there a member of your family who is a senior citizen? Ask that person if you could make a cassette or video tape of them talking to you about their life. Have the children help prepare questions about all the things that person experienced in their life, including things that the kids wouldn't even realize, like not having television, fast food restaurants, computers, etc. Ask what it was like to go to school, have children, work, etc. This will be a valued treasure in years to come. There is so much wisdom gained with age, it's important children experience this and see someone toward the end of their life thinking back on all they have experienced.

What Is Grieving?

When someone dies, people can feel very sad for a long time. This time of sadness is called grieving. People actually grieve over losses of all kinds: loss of a job, moving, divorce, death of a pet. The most important thing to remember about sadness that goes on for a long time is that all the feelings need to be expressed and heard. The family needs to support each person in feeling sorrow, helplessness, despair, hopelessness, anger, depression, guilt, even if it means just sitting quietly while someone expresses their feelings. Take time to talk about sadness. What things have happened in your family's life that have caused sadness? What is it that was lost? Take a few minutes to practice telling how you felt about it. Families need to be safe places for expressing sorrow as well as joy.

Remembering Our Pet Loss

We can get just as emotionally attached to a pet as we can to a person. After all, can you imagine a more sympathetic listener than a pet? Have each family member find or draw a picture, or write the name of some animal that either died or was lost that you miss. Get together and talk about that animal. Was there a burial? Do you remember it? Did the burial help you to say good-bye? What caused the death? How did you learn of the death? What did you do with the pet's collar...bowl...leash....cage...bed...toys? Did anyone else miss this pet as much as you? Even if the pet you loved has been gone a long time, they may still be missed. It's good to talk about and remember the animals we loved.

Let's Remember

When someone dies, there is usually a memorial service of some kind. This is so everyone can get together and remember that person's life. Why not have a little memorial celebration at home every so often to remember someone you loved? Begin by lighting a candle in honor of the person. Bring pictures, stories, anything you have that was theirs, letters or gifts from them, etc. Tell about funny things they did, vacations shared, important achievements, favorite phrases, movies, books and food they enjoyed. Sharing all of this together allows the person to live on in this moment's memories. You can also use this kind of celebration if someone dies and any part of the family is unable to attend the funeral.

Reflecting On Your Stage of Life

Life happens in stages. In between our first breath and our last, we go through infancy, childhood, adolescence, young adulthood, middle-age, and old age. Every stage has its challenges, privileges, lessons, and joys. Your children are sure to believe that the older you are the better life is because you can do what you want. Sometimes it is good to hear about each person's life from their point of view. For example, the oldest sister may seem to have the best life; she gets to stay up later, do more of the things she wants to, but she also has to care for the younger kids. The oldest may think that the youngest is so spoiled getting everything they want, and some may think Grandpa is luckiest because he gets to watch movies all day. Each person talk about the stage they are in right now and how it feels to them. As everyone listens, they will gain a new perspective on their own life as well as a better understanding of the struggles and joys other members of the family experience.

Plant a Memory Tree

When someone visits a graveside or cemetery, they often talk aloud to the person buried there. This is a normal and healthy thing. Why not plant a tree in the backyard in memory of your dead loved one? Talk to the family about making this a spot where everyone can visit when they want to be with the person who has died. As you care for the tree, or sit in its presence, think of the person you love and talk to them about how you feel. It sounds silly, but it can be such a relief to know there is a place to go, to be, to think, and to talk to the person missed so much.

Have a Remembrance Party

Who does your family miss? Why not enjoy remembering the deceased by hosting a party where everyone participates in his or her favorite activity? What activity brought this person his greatest joy in life: a hobby, a sport, an artistic expression, an everyday activity like a meal, watching TV, reading, making crafts? Imagine twenty people going fishing and reminiscing about Grandpa, or a slew of cooks in the kitchen making Aunt Dolly's famous spaghetti dish. Start planning, and make sure everyone has a job to do.

Saying Good-Bye

Anything you really cared about that used to be in your life, but is no longer present, deserves a formal farewell. It might be a person, pet, job, house, special place, object, or hobby. Saying good-bye to the things we loved that we no longer have can be an important part of emotionally letting go. Get together and have each family member draw a picture of someone or something meaningful to them that they never said good-bye to. When the pictures are all drawn, everyone share their feelings; then, have a good-bye celebration by burying them, burning them, putting them in a bottle and letting them float away, or anything else the group wants to do to say good-bye.

Daily Remembering

When someone we love has died, it can hurt daily. Get the family together to think of particular daily behaviors the deceased person enjoyed: tea at 9 a.m., a walk through the garden, feeding a pet, a book at bedtime, a personal habit, regularly catching the sports news. Consider ways to incorporate the remembered person's favorite behaviors into each of your daily lives as a way to remember them. This keeps their spirit alive in you.

Part Six:
Family Matters

Family History

What you are experiencing right this moment will tomorrow be called history. Every day in many ways, families share experiences and memories that live on in the minds of each family member and become family history. Each experience a person has shapes their view of the world, who they want to be, the work they want to do, and the way they relate to others. We all bring these experiences and views to our family experience. It is through this process of sharing individual and group experiences that families grow more and more connected to each other.

"What families have in common the world around is that they are the place where people learn who they are and how to be that way."
—Jean Illsley Clark

Matching Stories to Pictures

Family picture albums carry the images of events from the past. Not everyone in the family was present for every event pictured: they weren't born yet, were gone at camp, staying at Grandma's, etc. Take an evening to bring out the picture albums. Give everyone a little time to look through the albums for a few pictures that they don't know anything about. One at a time, present the chosen picture to the family while each person who knows something about the picture tells their story. Each person adds to the story until it is as complete as possible. Make sure you pull out a picture of something the younger children can talk about, like their own birthday party.

Start a Scrapbook

In the present moment, making a scrapbook may seem like just another thing to do, but what fun they are to look back on. Get everyone to participate in the making of a family scrapbook that has bits and pieces from each person's life. Tell everyone to start collecting memories of special events: announcements, programs, tickets, pictures, letters, invitations, etc. Plan an evening to start the scrapbook together. Write something at the beginning about your family, the year, general news, or anything that you all compose together. Put whatever memories that have been gathered into the book in a decorative way, making sure to add words describing the event. Store the book in a big box along with scissors, glue and colored paper. Scrapbooks are to be added to whenever someone wants to.

Different Versions

Because we are unique individuals, we each remember things differently. We may all be in the same place at the same time, but each one will have different memories of the event. Pick a past event for which everyone was present. Have someone start by telling the story in great detail from their point of view. After at least five minutes, the next person gets to tell their version. Isn't it fun to see how different people interpret different events? Make sure everyone laughs when they hear new versions instead of interrupting and telling the person they are wrong. In fact, there is only one rule to this game: there is no interrupting.

World Dinner

Talk together about all the countries of the world in which your family has roots. Have a world dinner to acknowledge and honor these countries. You may want to take one country at a time, and do one a month, until all of the families heritage has been learned about and experienced. First, pick out food that would be eaten in that country. Assign everyone something to do: help cook the dinner, read a poem or story about the country, sing a song, give a brief historical summary, talk about personal experience with this country. Work together to make this dinner a memorable experience!

Reflecting Back

Who you were two years ago is a piece of your personal history today, just as who you are today will be a piece of your personal history two years from now. Do you remember what your life was like two years ago? Get together and encourage everyone to share memories from that time. First, someone can share their memories, then everyone else can add what they remember about that person at that time. Keep all memories on the positive side; it is not helpful to say things like, "I remember how fat you were," or that "you had no friends." If the person wants to share their own negative things, let them do it.

Agenda Collection

What you choose to talk about today in family meetings will chart the family journey in weeks to come. Start a notebook where family meeting agendas can be saved. It's fun to look back on topics that were discussed. Certainly ten years from now the kids will get a laugh to see a whole meeting was devoted to why they couldn't have candy after school, sibling fighting, or summer vacation camps. It also helps children to get a sense of the work it takes to communicate and work as a family; it will be a reminder in their adult lives of the effort made in their family.

"When I Was Your Age" Stories

Kids love hearing what their parents were like at their age. Let your children tell you a story about their life now, their friends, toys, games, events, and hobbies. After the child is finished, each parent takes five minutes to tell about their life at the age of that child. Let each child have their turn, followed by the parents' stories of being that child's age. If the children like this storytelling, incorporate it into your everyday life whenever there is a chance: after the first day of kindergarten sit down and tell them what you remember about your kindergarten teacher, the first time a friend hurts their feelings tell them about your friend. Become a storyteller about your own life. It will create memories for your child.

251

Picturing Last Year

Every year of your family history has brought new and exciting experiences. What did last year bring your family? Pull together pictures representing last year's important events to assemble in a collage. Get a large picture frame and cut the pictures so that they all blend into a large view of the year. Let everybody help decide on the pictures to use and their placement. Glue them to a piece of cardboard the size of the frame, decoratively write the year, frame the collage, and hang it together.

252

A Space for Getting Attention

Remember how good it felt to get a lot of attention when you had "Show and Tell" in grade school? Why not pick a show and tell space in your house for everyone to display the things they are proud of? A shelf, tabletop, or a cabinet will do. Make sure to clear it off at the end of the week for new things to be displayed.

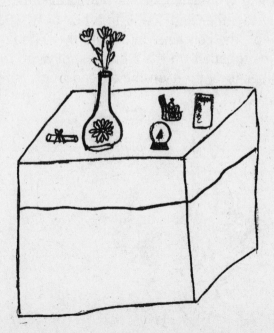

Making a Time Capsule

If you were to discover a time capsule your family had buried ten years ago, what would it contain? What if you make one today to be dug up ten years from now? A family time capsule is a collection of meaningful items representing family life today, this moment, right now. When it is opened it will say a lot about your family history. Let each person contribute a couple of things: today's newspaper, recent family meeting agenda, something written about life now, a picture, a tape recording. Bring everything together and seal it in a box or plastic container. Write the date clearly on the container and write the date you intend for it to be opened. Agree together on the storage spot and form a plan for how you will remember to open it on the agreed upon date.

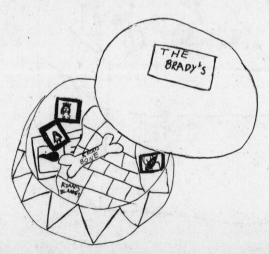

Make a Family Tree

Family trees are fun to draw. They give children a sense of where every-one fits in and makes them feel a part of something bigger than their immediate family. A good way to do a family tree is to give each child pieces of paper to decorate that represent women and men. Cut out cir-cles for women and squares for men, and have children decorate them and name them. Once all family members and relatives have a piece of paper with their name on it, start gluing the circles and squares to a large piece of paper. Talk about family members as you glue them to the paper. If you have no idea what a family tree looks like, go to the library and look for a reference book on genealogy and family history investigation.

Having Family Interviews

If you were interviewed by your family, you would feel people really wanted to know about you. That would make you feel very important. Asking questions about someone, listening to answers, and taking time to focus on just one person's life brings everyone closer together. Set up some time to conduct family interviews. Pick one person per week or whatever fits into the family schedule. Have everyone write down ten questions they plan to ask the person at the interview. Make sure to have a blank tape ready to record this piece of family history in the making. At the time of the interview, take turns asking questions and make sure not to rush the answers. You may want to set a time limit that you will stick with, and that everyone feels comfortable with, so that nobody feels more or less important in upcoming interviews.

Make a Family Crest

A family crest is a symbol your family can create using words and drawings. It represents the things important to everyone in your home. It could include pictures, symbols, words, historical ancestral information, etc. Include everything that makes your family unique and special. Hang the crest on the front door or someplace where everyone can see it.

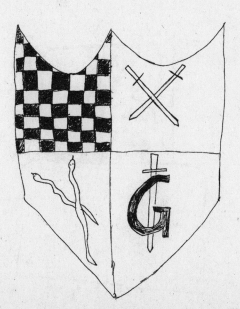

Home Movie Night

Shared memories create a family bond. If your family is lucky enough to have family movies, pick a night to watch them together. Make popcorn, relax, laugh, and remember all the memories you have shared as you watch yourselves in action. Why not make home movie night a family tradition?

Have a Family Journal

A family journal is different from a scrapbook because it contains more writing and description of individual events in each family member's life, rather than just pictures or other memorabilia. Get a large blank book to be used for the family journal. Write, draw, paste pictures, or record in any way your individual experiences of meaningful moments, unforgettable outbursts, personal challenges, successes and failures, special events, funniest moments, etc. The journal records what the family is feeling as well as what everyone is doing. Add to it often. You may wish to have an annual date when the whole family looks back through the journal and remembers.

Root of the Family

Buy a bulb to plant indoors, or a small tree to plant outdoors. Ask the children what roots do for a plant. The answer, of course, is that they support it, hold it up, and feed it. In fact, without roots, the tree or plant would die. Families have a root structure too, but family roots are things like honesty, kindness, cooperation, support, love, respect, and helpfulness. Without these things the family would fall. Talk about your family's root values. Draw a picture together of a tree or plant with roots showing. Place words you all agree to on the roots of the tree or plant. Hang the picture up where everyone can see it. As a symbol of your family's desire to strengthen their root system, plant a tree or bulb together. As everyone sees the tree or bulb growing they will be reminded of their family root values.

Write a Newsletter

Plan to write a newsletter after your family's next vacation. Even if you don't leave the house, you can still collect fun information about what the family is doing. Anyone who wants to can be a reporter looking for a story. The youngest might need an assistant to dictate their story to. Although your vacation may include the majesty of Mt. Everest or the magnificence of the Grand Canyon, your most inspired article might be about the anthill at your picnic, or the outrageous waitress that one night at dinner. It's as much fun planning your newsletter during your vacation as it is to create it once you're home. Don't forget to include drawings. Once written, print it up and send it out to friends and relatives. They'll love getting it in the mail.

Mom

The bond between mother and child is a magical, mystical, enduring, unconditional, and unexplainable phenomena. A mother is connected to her child's heart in a way that the child's feelings are felt even when the child is no longer a child. It is a great privilege and responsibility to be entrusted with the life of another, to be able to guide and listen, and to experience the unconditional love and trust that children so easily give. Within a mother's heart and life there must also be a place for herself where she retreats to feel refreshed and able to meet life's constant demands. A mother who devotes time to caring for her own needs teaches her children self-respect.

"Sometimes the strength of motherhood is greater than natural laws."
—Barbara Kingsolver

Knowing Yourself Through Journaling

As both a woman and mother in today's world, it is often hard to find time to think about thoughts, feelings, goals, dreams, fears, or life in general. A journal is a place where you can put all your thoughts—anything and everything about yourself. It will be a place you can turn to for comfort and inspiration. As you write, you will discover all sorts of things about YOU. The more you write, the more you will discover. A journal can be a friend, and a reminder of who you are, who you were, and who you are becoming. Buy a blank book and start writing today.

Acknowledging Your Own Goodness

Finish the following letter to yourself.

Dear (your first name),

I admire you as a woman and a mother and this is why...
I want you to know who the people are that you positively influence...
This is the impact you have on each of them...
I want you to understand that it makes a difference that you are exactly who you are because...

Reflect on these thoughts often.

Creating a Fantasy Day

Daydreaming, fantasizing, and relaxing are all things that can help you to find peace and happiness in your daily life, and they all use little time or energy. Start by writing down everything you would include in a fantasy day. There is no reality involved here, so let your imagination run wild. On this day, everything goes exactly the way you want it to, your smallest hopes, wishes, and needs are all fulfilled. Once you have thought about it for a while and have written it down, put on your favorite music, shut your eyes, and relax. Now, use your imagination and visualize every detail of that day. Take all the time you need and enjoy yourself. Who said daydreaming had to stop in elementary school!

Dreaming Up Solutions

When you have a problem, it helps to be open-minded and creative about solutions to it. Even if there is nothing you can do to change a problem right now, it helps very much to open your mind and thoughts to solutions of all kinds. Try this exercise in your journal. Write down the problem in the middle of the page, then, all around it, write every solution you can think of, no matter how silly, unrealistic, or seemingly impossible. Draw a line encircling all the solutions and the problem. Look at it every day for a while and don't be surprised when a workable solution pops up.

Getting Support for Mothering

Have you ever wondered why the earth is referred to as a mother? Maybe it's because the earth creates and sustains life just like human mothers. Being a mother is a big deal. It is a lifelong job and there is no real training course. So how do we answer the questions that come up daily, how do we know if we are making the right decisions or if we are good mothers? We must rely on our own intuition and each other. Take some time to write down the name of every mother you know. Next to the name, describe what you think makes her a good mother. Reflect on which qualities in other mothers are ones you also possess. Make a point to talk honestly to the other mothers in your life about the every-day worries and joys of mothering. We need to teach, support, and learn from each other.

Making Time for Creative Renewal

We all need some sort of creative outlet in our lives to feel happy. Sometimes, when life gets too busy, we forget to allow creative time. Take yourself back in time. Sit, close your eyes, and breathe deeply. Remember back into your childhood to the first time you remember feeling the joy of creative expression in something you said, did, made, or caused. Dwell for a moment on this memory and then move on in time from one creative memory to the next, eventually arriving at your life today. Is there a time in your life when you stopped creative expression? If so, why? How do you express that creative energy in your life today? Take some time to think about how you can find time to be creative, and don't forget that cooking a meal, decorating a table or room, and making up stories all count.

Clarifying Your True Responsibilities

Sometimes it's hard to determine what responsibilities are yours and what responsibilities are other family members'? To help yourself make this distinction, answer the following questions:

What things do I do:

...because everyone expects me to?

...even though the children are able to do them for themselves?

...because no one else will?

...because I don't like how others do them?

...because I'll feel guilty if I don't?

After you answer these questions, make a list of what you realize are your responsibilities. Explain to the rest of your family where you think you are taking responsibility for them, and what your new expectations are. You may even want to make a list and post it as a reminder. It may take time, but if you stick to doing only your responsibilities, you will find you have more time and less resentment, not to mention the fact that everyone in the family will grow in caring for themselves.

Changing Your Responses

Some days, when life's stresses get difficult, we respond in ways that we don't like and, in fact, wish we could take back. The way we respond under pressure can become a pattern that becomes difficult to change. There are two things to do when you aren't happy with the way you have handled a situation.

1. Close your eyes and review the situation in your head, trying to see all the little details. Once you have it clearly in your head, run the scene again, except this time change the way you act. Even though it is in your mind, it is a step toward being able to respond differently next time.

2. It is never too late to say you're sorry. A child will learn very much from this kind of modeling. You might say, "I had a very hard day today and I am so sorry that I yelled the way I did, it had nothing to do with how you were acting. Do you forgive me?"

Letting Go of Control

One of the most liberating concepts in life is being able to let someone do something their own way and be happy with it. In your home there are many jobs that need to be done, and most everyone has a specific way they want the job done. Give yourself a practice week at letting go and letting others accomplish tasks their own way. Start with something simple like the way the laundry is folded, or the way the dishes are loaded. For one whole week you are not allowed to correct anyone; they simply need to get the job done. At the end of the week, notice how it feels to let go. Look for other areas in your life where you could do the same thing. If you get good at this, you'll notice more time and much less stress in your day.

Cure for Loneliness

Mothers sometimes feel lonely and isolated; it's a natural thing considering how much time is spent in the company of children. You can be sure that if you are looking into the face of another mother, you are seeing someone who has felt the same way you do. Is there anything you are feeling that you think no one else is? Do you ever feel like your life just isn't going anywhere, that all you do is care for others, that you could be a better mother, or that no one understands you? Write your feelings down. Look at them each morning. Then, listen to other women as they talk and notice when they mention the same feelings. At least two times this week have the courage to be honest at these moments. This is how friendships are created.

Breath Hug

One of the best ways to relieve a tense feeling is with a long, relaxed hug. At the end of your day, when you hug your children goodnight, hold them for a long time and breathe until all your tension is dissolved. Children love feeling needed and loved. Make sure when you leave the room to thank them for the hug and tell them how good it made you feel. Breath hugs also work wonders when tension arises during the day and you want to make amends. There is something about holding and being held that brings peace.

Having a Circle of Friends

Every woman needs other female friends to talk to. Who are your friends and how do those relationships feel? Draw a large circle on a piece of paper representing a wheel. Draw your face in the center of the circle like the hub of a wheel. Draw spokes extending to the circle's edge. Write your friends' names on the spokes. The strength on your wheel comes from honesty. It is important to have a few spokes supporting your wheel—it helps life to roll smoothly. If you feel you don't have the kind of friends you can be honest with, and that you can trust with your feelings, it's time to look around and find women you want to know better. Making new friends is hard sometimes, but keep trying to connect. It will be worth it in the end.

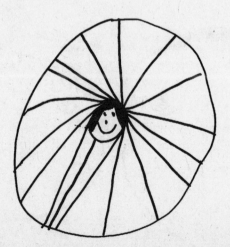

How We Affect Each Other

Starting at birth, each woman you have had in your life has taught you something. There are qualities you saw in them that you learned from, and there are things they did that you swore you would never do. Think about all the women who have touched your life. Write their names down, and next to their name write a short description of what you learned from them. After all their names are written, write your own name and what young women in your life will remember about you in years to come. Have the courage to tell the women in your life your true feelings, especially your daughters. Qualities we believe in and pass on give them strength to live according to their beliefs.

Today's Steps = Tomorrow's Life

Every step you take today is leading you somewhere. A year from today, your life will not be the same. Take a blank piece of paper and draw out your life today using words, figures, symbols, or pictures. Include things you like and things you don't like. On a second piece of paper, draw your life as you would like it to be a year from today. Date the drawings. Then answer the following question: What steps will I take to bring next year's picture to life? The steps you write down become the day-to-day goals you will accomplish. With each goal reached, you take a step toward a more fulfilled and happy tomorrow.

Dad

Dads seem invincible to their children. They are the ones who throw us high in the air as we giggle with delight, they hold us tight as we look into the campfire, they read us stories at night, they show us how the world works. Dads are strength, they are gentleness, they teach character, and they model discipline. Dads plan adventures, they set things up, they believe we can do it, and they encourage us to try again. In a father's eyes a child sees all the possibilities that await them out in the world. Holding a father's hand a child feels someone walking with them down life's path.

"Every day of my life has been a gift from him. His lap had been my refuge from lightning and thunder. His arms had sheltered me from teen-age heartbreak. His wisdom and understanding had sustained me as an adult."
—Nellie Pike Randall

Using a Journal

A journal is simply a record of thoughts, feelings, and life experiences. It gives the mind a place to put ideas to be thought about and worked through. If you have never kept a journal, it isn't too late; buy a blank book and start today. Make your first entry a description of your life right now. After you are done writing, go through the description and make a list, using single words, of all the things you like about your life as it is. Look at the things you don't like so much, and think of one way to change just one of them. Write as often as you can, if only for a few minutes at a time.

Reconnecting with Your Children

Sometimes parents have to work so hard to provide for the family that they lose touch with the day-to-day life and activities of their children. Take thirty minutes to spend with each child individually. The idea is for you to follow their lead, and play what they like to play. It is often tempting to have the child follow you around doing things you like, but that won't work in this activity. The idea is for you to get to know them better, to walk in their footsteps for a brief time. You will be surprised at how much energy and love your children will give you.

Being with Our Fathers

Fathering takes special skills and presents special challenges. Unfortunately, there is no college class in fathering, so dads have to learn as they go. It often helps to talk to other fathers. Much is often said about mothers having support groups, but what about fathers? There are many things fathers can share: experiences, advice, stories, outings, etc. Going to the zoo, park, swimming, or creek walking with another father is much more fun than going alone. You can use that time to talk and get support and ideas from each other. Today, take some time to think about one or two other fathers you know and plan to go someplace together with another father and all the kids between you. You may want to make a commitment to do this once a month.

Visualizing for Solutions

Whether it's work, a relationship with a child or spouse, a situation with a neighbor, or a vacation decision to make, apply the following technique to give your brain some different images to work with. Go to a place you won't be bothered, get comfortable, and relax. Start to imagine what you want the situation at work or in a family relationship to look like. See yourself hugging your spouse or playing with your child. Hear what you are saying to them. Take the problem and envision many solutions in your mind. Try to imagine what the outcome would be of each decision. Give your mind freedom to explore situations. If you have nothing in particular to work out, simply visualize your perfect day from beginning to end. Visualizing things can be very relaxing, and a good feeling usually follows, as if you had really experienced what you imagined.

Feeling Close

Never underestimate the power of touch—the power of a hug. For one week, hug your child and your wife at least once a day. A short squeeze doesn't really count; instead, count to ten slowly and really hold on. Older children may think they are too old for hugs, so you may have to start with shorter ones, or simply sit close to them and listen. The words "I love you" should be said as often as hugs are given!

Tower of Support

From the time you were born until now, there have been men in your life from whom you have received support. Brick by brick, imagine these men as forming a tower; you are always at the tower's top, and the men show up, starting at the bottom, in order of appearance in your life. Draw or sketch your tower. At the foundation, place the name of the first man in your life, written within a brick-shaped rectangle. In the brick next to his name, put a word there that represents the kind of support you got: encouragement, discipline, direction, laughter, affection, security, being there. Continue building your tower until you reach today, including every man in your life who has supported you in any way.

Realizing You Can Handle Anything

Every once in a while it is a good idea to prepare yourself for a possible problem. Sometimes it is easier to work through a problem and its solutions while not right in the middle of it; at least it trains your mind and gives you the power and belief that you could handle it should the problem ever occur. Here's how it works. Imagine something that you don't want to happen: loss of a job, death of a family member, a business mistake, a natural disaster, etc. Whatever the problem, zoom in on your personal strengths, skills, and resources that you would call on to survive this distress. Call on things like your ability to analyze, problem-solve, troubleshoot, and strategize, your patience, good judgment, moral fiber, persistence, and fortitude. See yourself working through the problem and handling it with ease.

Picture the Woman You Married

This is the day to think about the woman you married. Go through some family photos and pick out your favorite picture of your wife as a mother. Then pick your favorite picture of her as a woman. Gazing at these two pictures, sit for a while and think about the following questions:

- How much time do you spend with each of these women?
- How much support do you give to each of these women?
- What needs of yours are met by each of these women?

It is important to take the time to tell your wife often that you do see the many roles she plays in your family's life, and that you admire and love her.

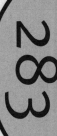

Lower Your Frustration Level

If your stress level is too high, your health and happiness are at risk. Make a list of all your responsibilities at home and at work. After you write down the responsibilities, go through the list and rate each one from one to five according to your level of frustration or stress, five being the highest and one being the lowest. Take a close look at the responsibilities rated four and five, and brainstorm some ways to lower the stress. Sometimes there are things you are doing that are not your responsibility at all. Take time to talk to your spouse and children about how you plan to lower your stress level, and how they can help you.

Getting Needs Met

Can you remember what you needed from your father when you were a child? Think about your childhood needs that were met, as well as your childhood needs that were not met. What you needed from your father is probably very similar to what your children need from you. Select a favorite picture of each one of your children and look at each one individually while you think about what that child needs from you. Pick one need each child might have and plan something specific to meet it. Don't get overwhelmed trying to change too many things at once. Just take one step at a time.

Dreaming Up Your Future

Have you ever thought what you want your life to look like ten years from now? Organize your thoughts around home, family and friends, work, finances, and recreation. Think of it as a picture of your future. After you have thought of a few ideas, begin to write them down. Look at what you have written, then outline the steps you need to take in each area to reach your ten year dreams. Look at this often as a reminder of where you are going.

Your Wildest Dreams

Having a mental picture of abundance not only makes for cheery days, but some say it sets the stage for great things to materialize. It's just plain fun to think about dreams coming true. Shut your eyes and let your imagination run wild as you fantasize how you would spend ten million dollars. Write it down if you want to.

Parent to Parent

When you parent with another person, you enter a kind of partnership of respect. You may not always have the same views, but you learn to accept differences of opinions and you learn to compromise on small and large issues. The way parents work out problems, the way they communicate, and the way they love each other is a child's first observation of how people get along in the world. Most children see and feel everything. They are like sponges soaking in everything their parents do. Parents who work together as a team with love and respect give their children a safe and trusting place to grow.

"Whatever you would have your children become, strive to exhibit in your own lives and conversation."
—Lydia H. Sigourney

Listen to Each Other

Do this activity the same time each evening for one week and see what happens. It's very simple. One of you talks for ten minutes about whatever you want while the other person listens. No comments are made, and no subject is out of bounds. Speak about everyday things, the kids, your dreams, problems, fears, love, whatever you feel like. When ten minutes are up, switch roles. Listening and paying attention to someone is the greatest gift we can give them.

Partners Support Each Other

Partnership is when you each do the most of what you do best. It's not about being equal in all things. It's important to help each other out in areas where help is needed. Take some time for each of you to list all the things you do each day. Circle the ones you would like some help in. Discuss the ways you might get help: being willing to help each other out, pitching in, taking over if asked, acknowledging something done well, etc. Listen with an open heart and a creative mind. Some solutions may seem impossible at first, but with a little imagination they may grow into a possibility. Each person can only give so much support. If you have to say "no" to each other, at least make an effort to give daily encouragement in the area for which help was asked.

Similar Views or Respect Differences

Take time to sit down with your partner and simply discuss your opinions on a subject that includes both of you: how time is spent together, responsibilities, hobbies or activities, future plans, raising the children, social life, extended family, or household chores. Since both of you come from different backgrounds, your opinions may be very different, or very much the same. When parenting together, there are two choices: either have similar views, or accept each person's right to a different view. Knowing and respecting each other's views will make you a better team; it will also give the kids a great model of how to accept and respect people's differences.

Element of Surprise

Surprises can instantly turn an ordinary day into a special one! When was the last time you surprised your partner? Do you know what kind of surprises would put a smile on their face? Let your imaginations run wild as you share with each other the most outlandish, unlikely, or loving kinds of surprises that would please you. A few weeks after this lively discussion, plan a surprise. What a fun way to enjoy and appreciate each other!

Appreciating Each Other

Appreciation needs to be heard loud and clear. Here's a fun game that voices your appreciation. Pick a code word from nature: mud, bluebird, sky, rose, ocean, etc. For one day, each time you appreciate something your partner does, say the code word. They get three guesses to figure out what they've done that you are appreciating. If they can't guess, tell them very specifically what you liked about their behavior.

Family Goals

Have you ever sat down with your partner and discussed the commitments to your family that you both feel strongly about? What are your goals? What steps are you taking together to meet these goals? Make a list of all the agreed-upon commitments that guide you in day-to-day life. Here are a few examples:

We are committed to making our home beautiful, functional, comfortable, ecological, casual, tidy, creative...

We are committed to the development of each person's special talent and ability
to educating our children well
to building character
to providing for our children the best we can
to love and understanding in our family
relationships
to our health

There is strength in agreement and focus. Take one of these areas and make it the focus in both your lives for a week.

Shared Memories

Do you remember the joy and excitement of your wedding day, the hope you had, the belief in each other and your life together? Set a special date to share that memory again. Get out the wedding scrapbooks or watch your wedding video together. Remember what you felt, wondered, dreamed of, questioned, and expected the day you were united. Memories are created each day of our lives. Don't forget to keep building new memories.

Open-Hearted Arguing

Everybody argues, it's part of family life. There is one guideline to follow during an argument: keep an open heart. This means you continue to care about the other person while you argue. Pick a topic that you consistently disagree on and discuss it for ten minutes with an open heart; words, facial expressions, tone of voice, and gestures all carry the message that you care about and are interested in what the other person has to say. Everyone likes to win, but if you can care less about winning and more about understanding each other, your relationship will grow stronger and you will be setting a great example for your children to follow. Make a commitment to becoming open-hearted arguers.

Share Your Dreams

Each of you take a piece of paper, and without trying to be realistic, write down everything you want out of the rest of your life. Include career plans, purchases, skills and talents you want to develop, hobbies to pursue, projects, travel plans, education, and any special contribution you would like to make. Once you have finished your individual lists, start sharing them with each other. Using a large sheet of paper, begin listing the dreams that you both agree to put on your joint list. If your partner agrees to have your dream on the joint list, that does not mean an obligation to do anything about it. If you agree to your partner's dream of a vegetable garden, you are not obligated to pull weeds; if your partner wants to add a room onto the house, you're not obligated to pound nails. What you are obliged to do is support and encourage each other in reaching your dreams. Enjoy dreaming up a life together that is filled with the best that both of you can imagine.

Play with Each Other

Make a date with each other for a morning, an afternoon, or an evening, with only one purpose in mind: to have fun! The one rule to follow on this fun date is to not do or talk about anything serious. Do whatever you want, go wherever you want to, as long as you don't bring along the part of you that's the mature, concerned, responsible, and serious adult. Play with each other like children. Sometimes in the midst of so much adult responsibility its hard to remember the tremendous fun and joy we can have just being together.

Siblings

Siblings have the unique opportunity of going through life together, growing into adulthood side by side, sharing the same parent, and sharing life experiences. Children don't always see the great value in having a sibling. To a child, a sibling can be a friend one day and an enemy another. A sibling can share a great secret or give a great secret away. A sibling can be at their side in distress, or can lead the attack party. As parents, the best we can do is to encourage communication, love, and respect, trusting that there is a river of love that floats beneath them even when they are not in the same boat. So even if today a child cannot see the value of their sibling, someday they will.

"Both within the family and without, our sisters hold up our mirrors: our images of who we are and who we can dare to become."
—Elizabeth Fishel

Brother Day, Sister Day

We celebrate Mother's Day and Father's Day each year; why not invent a Brother and Sister Day? Get your family together and pick a day sometime during the year that you will keep as a special brother day or sister day. On that day, tell your brother or sister how much you appreciate them: make them something, serve them breakfast in bed, do one of their chores, plan a special outing or whatever you can think of. Make sure to have a separate Brother Day and a separate Sister Day. Mom and Dad can join in by sending their own siblings a special card on that day, and by telling their children all the special things they can remember about their sibling.

Working with Sibling Rivalry

Have you ever thought that there might be certain benefits that children gain through sibling rivalry? Things like self-defense, thinking on their feet, problem-solving, resolving differences, tolerating being excluded, managing frustration, getting along even when they don't want to, and much more. If a parent can accept that sibling rivalry is normal, and can tolerate it without stepping in, then the situation might change. Here's what you do when you hear trouble brewing: Say, "I've learned it's normal that you (argue, fight, insult) each other. I'm going to let you resolve this. If you need my help, I'm here." Do this for a few days and see what happens.

Waving the Peace Flag

How often do you feel like there's a small war going on in your home? Children's warlike behavior is intended to protect territory and possessions, get revenge, get attention, and to drum up support for their position. It is important that a child also have a way to not engage in warlike behavior against siblings. Get everyone together and talk about peaceful solutions based on listening to one another's feelings, problem-solving, and respect for one another's rights. Using a rectangular cloth of any sort, design a peace flag together, using markers, fabric paint, felt, etc. Talk about the following concept: if someone picks up the peace flag, it means that they want to talk instead of being attacked. Put the peace flag in a central location so it can be reached easily. Promote peace.

Valuing Individual Differences

Once children start going to school, they start to notice things that the other children do, wear, say, or like. It seems they start wanting to become similar to others. Or younger kids might look at older siblings and want to do the same things just because their brother or sister likes to do them. Now is a good time to talk about how each person is uniquely different, and that differences make life interesting. Get everyone together and write each family member's name on their own sheet of paper. Taking one person at a time, everyone contribute in describing that person. Write a physical description, their unique qualities, talents, likes and dislikes, hobbies, or anything else that describes that person. Do this for each person in the family. Put all the papers in a row and marvel at the differences and how wonderful it is to be different.

Supporting differences in family members helps children accept differences in other people outside the home, helping to create a child with an open mind!

Famous Siblings

Sometimes brothers and sisters think that their sibling is nothing but trouble: they have to share clothes, share parents, share attention, and share the bathroom. It might be a fun project to have your children search for famous siblings and read about them: the Wright brothers, the Brontë sisters, Venus and Serena Williams, or Prince William and Prince Harry. It's important that siblings know that they will continue to grow up, and someday they will be close friends with their sibling, even though it may not seem like it right now. Their sibling can be someone they admire and look up to. Talk about how important it is to support each other, whether you're doing something great in the world like inventing airplanes or writing books, or simply becoming great human beings!

Being Dishonest with Dicey Feelings

This is a game for only two siblings to play, and not for a whole group. If more than two play, or if too many people are watching, one or the other sibling may get their feelings hurt, or feel ganged up on. The idea is to have each sibling express to the other their honest feelings about them, both good and bad. Use one die and set this book in the middle of the table so that the children can refer to it. Take turns rolling the die. Whatever number is rolled, follow the instructions below:

- Tell your sibling something you like that they do.
- Tell your sibling something you don't like that they do.
- Tell your sibling one thing you are proud of them for.
- Tell your sibling something they do that embarrasses you.
- Tell your sibling something about them that you are jealous of.
- Tell your sibling something they do that hurts you.

Kids' Club

Instead of trying to explain what a kids club is to your children, give them this book, open to this page, and let them read it themselves.

Hi Kids! Do you ever feel like parents make all the decisions, get to work out all the problems, pick outings, and generally run the house? Here is your chance to organize yourselves. Even if there are only two of you, it still makes a difference if you both agree and set goals together; parents are more likely to accept ideas that kids agree on. Here's what you do. Pick a meeting time for just you kids, maybe two times a week. Write an agenda listing what you want to talk about at the meeting. Leave it someplace where only you kids can find it, but your parents can't. Make up membership rules, a slogan, a club name, and a secret code. Everyone has to promise not to tell the adults what is discussed. If a decision is made that needs to brought up to the whole family, then schedule a meeting for everyone. Have fun and be creative; do fund-raisers, plan surprise parties, pick family outings, have secret pals, etc.

Telling Your Own Story

As siblings go through life together, they all experience many of the same things: the first day of school, learning to ride a bike, playing a particular sport, first overnight sleep-over, having the same teacher. It's fun to get together and talk about those experiences as a group. Pick an experience that most all of the children have had, and let each one tell their own story about their unique experience. As each child tells their story, the others will realize that it's possible to share the exact same event, yet experience it differently. They will learn something about point of view. Point out that, although everything in their life will be interpreted through their own mind, different people see things differently and that it's simply their point of view. Pick a new subject and tell new stories. This is a great way for the kids to get to know each other better and to learn to accept differences in opinion.

Telling Family Stories

Unless you were an only child, you have stories to tell your children about your own life with your brothers and sisters. These stories need to be passed down and told. They hold many lessons and laughs, and give your kids an insight into who their parents, uncles, and aunts are and what their life was like. Plan a storytelling night, and if possible invite that brother or sister over to participate in the storytelling. Talk about how you played, laughed, fought, embarrassed each other, worked together, cried together, and how you all lived together as a family. Tell them what your parents did when you did something wrong. Tell them what having the same teacher was like. You will be amazed how hard your kids will listen trying to find out all the details. They will also like watching you and your sibling disputing the facts.

Siblings Sharing Thoughts

Make a copy of this page for each child in your family to fill out about each of their siblings.

_____ thoughts on _____ Date _____
(first name)   (first name)

	Always	Sometimes	Never
s/he is proud of me	___	___	___
s/he shows up for my activities	___	___	___
s/he plays with me	___	___	___
s/he shares stuff with me	___	___	___
s/he is happy when I'm successful	___	___	___
s/he leaves me alone if I ask	___	___	___
s/he respects my property	___	___	___
s/he listens to me	___	___	___
s/he laughs with me	___	___	___
s/he keeps my secrets	___	___	___
s/he takes my side	___	___	___
s/he helps me when I'm in trouble	___	___	___

Before the kids start, make sure that they understand that this is not to be a mean thing. It is for each child to see where they are helping their sibling and where they are hurting them. This should only be done if children all agree that they want to be evaluated. Help them if they need it, and sit with the two of them as they read it to each other.

Putting the Kids on Stage

Kids usually love to be the center of attention. Give them a chance to take center stage together as they put on some sort of performance. They could write a play and perform it, do a puppet show, re-enact a moment of family history, do a song or dance, a comedy act, magic show, or anything else they come up with. They could also make their own tickets and refreshments. Working together on a fun project deepens sibling's appreciation of each other. Your only job as parents is to be entertained and enjoy the show.

Older to Younger

There will never be a generation gap if the desire to listen and understand is present. When we value each others' ideas, experiences, and wisdom, it is possible to learn from each other. Older people have life experiences the young are waiting to experience, and young people see the world through fresh eyes. There is so much to share if hearts and minds remain open to the idea that each human being, no matter their age, has something to offer.

"I have found the best way to give advice to your children is to find out what they want and then advise them to do it."
—Harry S. Truman

Giving What You Need

Can you close your eyes and remember yourself at your child's age? Can you remember the things you needed and wanted most from your parents? Think about how you felt as a child. Spend some time with your child, giving to them the things you wanted and needed most from your parents. Chances are they need the same things you did!

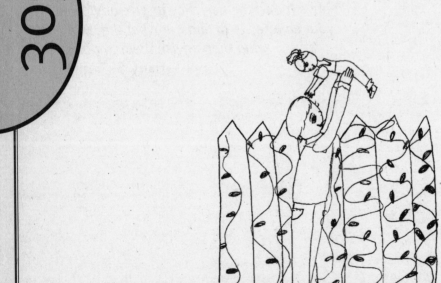

Listening to What Children Really Think

Have you ever thought of interviewing your child to get their opinions on things? Ask your child if they would have time for an interview. You may even want to use a microphone and tape recorder like a real interview! Ask questions like the following: What do you think you want to be when you grow up? Do you think you want to do just one thing or a lot of different things? What are they? Do you think you want to get married and raise a family? Why or why not? How will you treat your children? Where will you want to live? What kind of a home? Will you travel? Where to? What will your friends and neighbors be like? Will you have hobbies? Pets? What do you want the world to be like? Be sure to remember where you store this tape. It could be a fun gift on the child's 21st birthday.

Most Precious Gift

Most parents fill out baby books that list the baby's basic facts. Then come the school books full of more information. None of these books express the personality of the child. Get a blank book and begin writing to your child about who they are. Every so often, take the time to write about how your child is doing, how you are being challenged by parenting the child, what the child is doing well and what they are having trouble with, current joys and delights, your relationship with them, funny things the child does, words they say, how they explain things, interactions with their siblings, what their daily life is like, struggles in the family. Write everything you feel about this child and your life together. Plan to give this book to your child when they grow up and leave home. Upon reading it, the child will understand themselves better and feel your undying love for them.

Play Make-Believe

Adults need to play and have fun too. The more fun you have, the better your outlook on life and the healthier you are in general. If you didn't have adults to play with when you were a child, you may have gotten the idea that play was only for children. Start your play experience with a game of make-believe. Ask the child in your life to show you how. Whatever you do, pretend you're doing something else. If you go to the market, pretend you're on a treasure hunt. If you're at a playground, pretend you're on a deserted island. If you're taking a walk, pretend you're lost in the forest. Have fun.

Be Eager to Talk

Do you ever feel like you ask your child the same questions every day? How was your day? What did you do at school? Who did you play with? Today, instead of asking the same questions, trigger their imagination by telling them something odd, unusual, exciting, or interesting that you experienced recently. Watch their little face for reactions as you are talking, giving them all the time they need to come back, eager to talk, with comments and questions. After all, they aren't the only ones with interesting lives!

From Younger to Older

Have you ever taken advice from your child? One morning before dress-
ing, ask your child's advice on what to wear that day. Really listen,
don't try to change their mind, respect their opinion, and for just this one
day, wear whatever they suggest. An adult who is able to receive an
opinion or advice from a child creates a special bond of respect.

The Moral of the Story Is...

You can teach children moral lessons by telling them stories about experiences you have had. In the thick of a difficult situation, a child is too vulnerable to hear moralizing, and needs support instead. But remember when the next day comes, make up a lighthearted story about yourself as a child that describes the same or a similar situation. Tell the story in a casual, matter-of-fact way: "I was just thinking about when I..." Try to tell the story without referring to the previous day's incident.

Learning to Visualize the Ideal

When a young person comes to you with a problem, you can give them a tool for life by helping them visualize a solution. First, listen carefully to what the problem is.

Then ask the child, "What would have happened, or what would it have been like, if things had been just the way
you wanted?" Have the child shut their eyes and visualize (see a detailed picture in their mind). Now talk your child through the situation as they would have wanted it to be. Ask questions like, "What are the kids wearing? What kind of a day is it? What is happening and what are people saying? How are you feeling?" By teaching a child how to visualize, you will give them a very positive inner experience to draw on when solving future problems.

Sending Little Love Notes

What a wonderful surprise to wake up in the morning to a message of love. Before you go to bed tonight, write a little love note to your child and leave it on the breakfast table where it will be read in the morning. Write about something you noticed they did well that day, and tell them how much you love them.

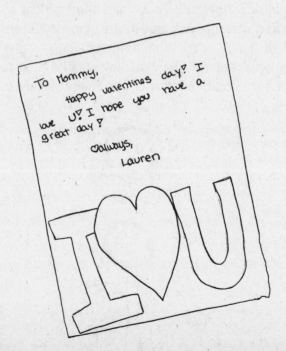

Giving the Gift of Respect

One way children learn to respect others' opinions is by having their own opinion respected. Here's a way you can give this special gift. Set up a time with each of your children to give them a copy of this form to fill out. Sit with them as they fill out the form, and listen carefully to their opinions.

_____ date	_____ name (mom/dad/other)	always	sometimes	never
	• listens to my problems	_____	_____	_____
	• loves me no matter what	_____	_____	_____
	• plays with me	_____	_____	_____
	• helps me out	_____	_____	_____
	• comes to my special events	_____	_____	_____
	• pays attention to me	_____	_____	_____
	• tries to be fair	_____	_____	_____
	• tells me the truth	_____	_____	_____
	• shares about themselves	_____	_____	_____
	• lets me be myself	_____	_____	_____
	• leaves me alone enough	_____	_____	_____

Please feel free to make as many copies of this page as you need.

Taped Esteem

Children believe what they hear about themselves. Make a cassette tape to give to your child, including the most positive things you can say about them. While making the recording, look at one of your fondest pictures of the child. With love and enthusiasm say things like, "I really like it when you...I appreciated the way you...It always makes me smile when you...I think it's wonderful that you...I'm awfully glad that you...You are a special person because..." Whether the child listens to it while falling asleep, or at a time of difficulty, the taped reassurances will affect their mood. It really is true that we become what we believe about ourselves.

Family Meetings

A scheduled family meeting communicates to your children that the family truly cares about everyone's opinion and wants to work as a team in making family decisions. Family meetings might be a child's first experience working with other people to make a decision, to discuss a problem, or to share thoughts. It also gives each child an opportunity to be a leader. Having an established and dependable place where each person knows they will be heard builds trust within the family system.

"If you know you are on the right track, if you have this inner knowledge, then nobody can turn you off...regardless of what they say."
—Barbara McClintock

Mastering the Technical Details

Once you have decided you want to have family meetings, pick a time for your first one. At this first meeting, discuss the structure of the meetings.

1. Set a regular meeting day and time. Weekly one hour meetings should be a goal to work toward.
2. The basic rule about leaders is that anyone who can read can lead the meetings, so give all who qualify the chance.
3. Make the agenda. Pick a central location where the agenda will be posted. The agenda is simply a blank piece of paper that people write on during the week. Only things written on the agenda will be discussed.

At this first meeting, talk about why it is important for your family to meet regularly.

Creating the Agenda

What do you write on the family meeting agenda? Anything a family member wants to discuss: changes in family rules, a problem they have, school, work, food, etc. Negative complaints about a specific family member should not be listed; instead, write the general topic. For example, instead of saying, "Debbie is hitting me," the topic should be, "Rules about hitting." The group can then go over the rules and consequences without starting an argument. It is important that each person takes time to add to the agenda during the week, because once the meeting starts, new topics cannot be added. This keeps the meeting from going on endlessly. If the topics discussed bring up new discussions, encourage family members to write them at the top of the next meeting's agenda. Store each week's agenda in a binder. It will be a nice record documenting family decisions and goals. Respect each person's right to discuss what is important to them; no making fun or saying, "that's stupid!"

Building Leadership Skills

Every person who can read should get the chance to be the family meeting leader. Leadership jobs include reading the topics off the agenda in the order they are written, calling for a vote if one is required, opening and closing the meeting, and keeping the discussion moving along. Young leaders may find all of these jobs difficult to do at once, so they should have an adult assistant. The young leader can read off the agenda while the adult helps direct the meeting. The leader should also make sure each person gets a chance to talk, and that interruptions are kept to a minimum.

Learning the Meeting Format

It is important for each family meeting to start off with a positive feeling. Take five to ten minutes and have each person do one of the following:

- Say the best thing that happened to them that week.
- Say something that they appreciate about each family member, including themselves.
- Say something nice that was done for them, or that they did for someone else.
- What they are most looking forward to in the coming week.

The idea is to talk and get to know each other better in as positive a way as possible. The middle of the meeting, which should last thirty to forty-five minutes, is when the agenda is read by the leader, one item at a time, with a brief discussion following each topic. After the agenda has been read, the leader makes sure there will be a leader for the next week. End the meeting with a closing time that might include a group hug. Share some sort of refreshment after the meeting.

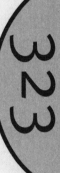

323

Creating Family Rules

Every family has rules, but does every family member know what they are? Take one family meeting to discuss, agree on, and list the family rules. Do your best to make sure the rules are understood and agreed upon. Family rules are statements that express how things are "supposed to go" in your family. For example, dinner is at 6:00, everyone eats dinner together, everyone eats dinner at their convenience, we clean up after ourselves, no TV during meals, call home if you have a problem, chores first and play later, no hitting or name calling, respect other people's belongings, etc. Post the list of rules where everyone can see them, or make a copy for each person to post in their own room. Simply acknowledging the rules makes group living more enjoyable.

Giving and Getting Family Support

Family is the first place we learn about supporting others. Devote a whole meeting to the concept of giving support and getting support. One at a time, each person simply say what's important to them in their life at this time. Everyone else, listen carefully to the person who is talking, then as a group ask, "What can we do to support you in this?" Discuss what each person could do to help support the talking person. You may even want to write down some ideas. Even very young children can talk about things, like a pet, and maybe the support they need is help cleaning a cage. Be creative in helping children decide what is important and what they need help with. Listen for five to ten minutes per person. Make sure everyone has a turn.

Being a Very Important Person

How exciting to be called a very important person for a whole week. Let the youngest person be VIP first. Place the VIP's picture on the refrigerator, or some place everyone sees it. The family can create their own VIP privileges. Some ideas are:

• Each night the VIP gets to share something at dinner.
• Before bed each person hugs the VIP warmly.
• The VIP gets to pick a designated meal.
• The VIP gets a note of encouragement or love from each family member sometime during their VIP week.
• The VIP gets interviewed by family (#256)
• At a family meeting, each family member says something they like about the VIP.

Finding Solutions to Problems

Problem-solving is a skill each family member needs to learn and use. Some people call it conflict resolution. Here's how it works:

1. First identify the problem (for example, children arguing all the time).
2. Have each person say whatever they need to say about the problem: "I can't do homework when there is yelling," "I can't concentrate on my work," "It scares me when I hear so much arguing."
3. Make a big list of possible solutions to the problem. List them, no matter how silly they sound. For example: the arguing people have to write about the problem to each other; when arguing starts, the two people have to go out in the garage with the door closed; the two arguing can ask another family member to mediate the argument, etc.
4. One by one, go through each solution, and when you find one that everyone can agree on, you have found your solution.
5. Make sure that solution is used during the next week as a consequence to arguing.

Problem solving takes time; it takes love and understanding. This is a skill your children will use for the rest of their lives. It is worth spending time on!

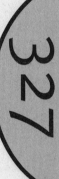

Having an Emergency Meeting

Once family meetings are a habit in your house, and communication, problem solving and listening skills have been taught, you can call an emergency meeting if needed. Anyone can call an emergency meeting if they need support, or they have a decision that needs to be made immediately, or they have something exciting to announce. Sit calmly together listening to everything. Before making any major decision, sit sixty seconds in silence.

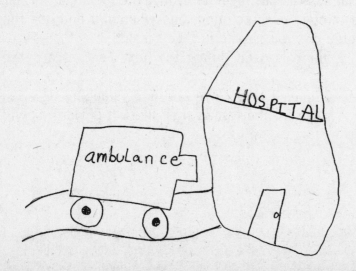

Closing the Meeting with Love

The way you leave each other from the family meeting is very important. Don't ever let anyone storm off mad or upset. There are many ways to end the meeting. Your family should decide on its own closing. Here are a few ideas to help you think:

- Stand in a circle holding hands. The leader starts by squeezing the person's hand to their right. The squeeze goes around the whole circle.
- Each person could say what they are looking forward to in the upcoming week.
- Have a big group hug.

After the meeting, have a snack together.

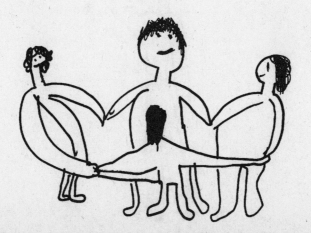

Making It Your Own

All of the activities in this chapter are guidelines. They are ideas to help your family meetings succeed. Ultimately, your family meetings are yours, so take a meeting to discuss what everyone likes or dislikes about the format you have tried. If at any time your meetings take on the atmosphere of a trial, full of blaming or judgment, STOP! Remember, the meetings are supposed to be a source of support and love.

Part Seven:
Having Fun Together

Fun and Games

It's so important that families take time out to play together. Experiencing laughter, fun, and adventure creates memories that will be brought up year after year with a smile. Family is a place where shared experiences bond lives together for years and years.

"A happy family is but an earlier heaven."
—John Bowring

Remembering to Play

Children know how to play, it is their life's work. If adults watch them and join in, they can stay young at heart and learn so much about their child. Today, build a fort together. Remember the days when the trees, the garage, or an old box meant hours of play for you? Tell your child you will follow their lead and be their building assistant. Build the fort wherever you want to, inside or out. Once the fort is built, play together in it for a while. Take a picture while in it and hang it up to remind you to keep a playful attitude in your heart.

Plan a Mini-Vacation at Home

When you're thinking about time off, don't ignore the option of staying home and doing something unusual. Get everybody together to plan a mini-vacation at home. It's tricky because you'll almost need to pretend you are somewhere else while you're at home. For this purpose, name your home a hotel. Select restaurants in the area where you'll be eating. Choose nearby places of interest or events to attend. Don't do any routine chores. Think about hiring a teenage neighbor to provide maid service while you're out. Unplug the phone. Call out for pizza and pretend it's room service. Send postcards to friends and relatives. Take pictures. Vacations are for having fun no matter where you are.

Storytelling with Favorite Words

Enjoy a storytelling session using favorite words contributed by each person. This is how it works. Sit around a table with pencil and paper in hand. Each person says one of their favorite words and everyone writes the words down on their own paper. When ten words are thought of and written down, begin the storytelling. Take a few minutes for each person to make up their own story in their mind, using the ten words. When everyone is ready, start sharing your stories. The stories can be written down or made up as you go.

Passing on Your Favorite Games

Some evening the adults get to tell the kids all about the games they played when they were children. If specific experiences can be remembered, talk about them: things done with their aunts, uncles, family, friends. Tell them who taught you the game, why you liked it, and who you played it with. If the game is still sold in stores, get one and teach it to them; if not, teach them a favorite card game.

Playing with Dance

Get everyone involved in this group dance. Put on some lively music that everyone likes and clear a big open space. Someone start as the leader by making up some fun and funny steps that everyone can follow along with for a few minutes. When the leader taps someone else on the shoulder, everyone follows along with their dance steps for a few minutes before the next leader is tapped. Keep going as long as you like. If everyone likes the concept of dancing, you could even put a few steps together and do the dance together.

Things to Do While Driving

Start to develop a bunch of games everyone knows that can be played while driving in the car. Give each person the job of finding a car game or making one up. Whoever brought the game is responsible for knowing the rules and teaching them, and keeping score if required. Simple games like the following ones get everybody involved, and bring more fun and togetherness into being on the road:

- Twenty questions (Pick a person, place, or thing and people get to ask twenty questions before they guess what it is. Questions can only be answered with yes or no.)
- Free associations (Say a word. Next person says any word that comes to mind. Keep going, like this: bird...fly...airplane...vacation...etc.)
- Add-on story-telling (Someone starts a story. After a few minutes, they say "Pass." The next person adds onto the story for a few minutes. Keep going.)

Wolf in the Woods

At the end of the day, some of us are too tired to play. Here's a game that lets everyone rest and still have fun! Pretend the living room is a forest with one wolf and several other animals running around. One person is the wolf, everyone else pretends to be other forest animals. The other animals lie on the forest floor perfectly still with their eyes wide open. No moving is allowed except for breathing, blinking, and eye movement. You're out of the game if the wolf catches you moving in any other way. The wolf is allowed to try to get the other animals to move any way she can without touching them: by making funny faces, strange sounds, or telling them jokes. The winner of this game gets to be the next wolf.

Play at Work

To kids, work and play are the same thing. With this in mind, plan a family work day with fun in mind. Let the imagination turn every bit of household work into play: mowing the lawn becomes giving Mother Earth a haircut, emptying the trash becomes feeding the trash monster, dusting furniture becomes removing finger-painting canvases, etc. Play games as you clean: give each person a job to do then set a timer and the first person done wins, or when the timer rings everyone has to go on a treasure hunt to find a hidden snack. Put on some music and dance your way to a clean house. The idea is to make it fun in any way you can, allowing everyone to help beautify the house with good attitudes.

Letting Yourself Dream

Dreaming is fun to do. So often as adults we keep reality too much in mind and don't give our minds space to wander. Get out some paper, pencils, markers, etc. Everyone sit down together at the table and begin to draw your dream home. This does not have to be architecturally accurate or even look like a house. Simple lines can represent the horse barn, or an attic library. Draw the outside, the inside, or both. Take some time to let everyone finish, then give everyone a chance to talk about their drawing. How would they furnish their rooms? What would the colors be? Would it be in the country or the city? Dream big!

Entertaining Each Other

If there aren't at least four people in your family, recruit grandparents, aunts and uncles, neighbors, and friends so you can make up a skit together. Split into two groups. Each group make up a skit about something humorous involving family life. Take 15 to 30 minutes to prepare. You can arrange furniture to set the stage, make use of props, do some simple costuming, make up, special effects, etc. Make it as elaborate or as simple as you want. When everyone is ready, perform the skits for each other.

Guess Who's Leading

This is a mirroring game where everyone imitates the movements of the leader. To practice for the game, the oldest family member takes the role of leader first. As the leader moves, everyone else does exactly the same movements at the same time. Sitting in a circle, the leader makes slow movements with their arms, legs, and head, and everyone else imitates the same slow movements. Let each person lead for a few minutes. That was practice. Now the fun begins. One person, called the investigator, leaves the room while the rest secretly decide on a leader. When the Investigator is called back, the movement game begins again. The object is for the Investigator to discover who is being the leader. Once the leader is discovered, that person becomes the next Investigator and the game goes on.

Postcard Memories

Wherever you go these days, you can find a postcard with a picture of that place on it. Make it a family tradition to buy a postcard at every spot you visit. Each time you buy one, somebody writes a little note on the back. Include the date, special memories or events, and the names and ages of all the travelers present. Mail the postcards home to yourselves and collect them in a special box. Whenever anyone wants to, you can play "Pick a Postcard." Whatever card you pick, tell your story about what's pictured on the postcard.

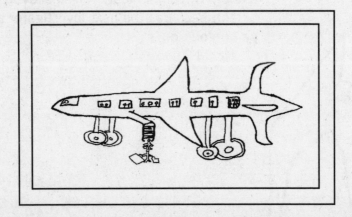

Humor

There is no sound like laughter to lighten the mind's load. Families who value humor, who can laugh together, and who enjoy the sound of fun, have the only medicine that money cannot buy. Those who befriend laughter learn early not to take life so seriously, seeing the humor in everyday events and experiences. Laughter can transform any moment into a friendly, fun, and easy place.

> *"Laughter can be more satisfying than honor; more precious*
> *than money; more heart-cleansing than prayer."*
> —Harriet Rochlin

Think of Silly Things

Humor is one thing that can turn a day around. It can transform stress, anger, sadness, or frustration into endless giggles. How do we teach children to find humor in life, to laugh, to not take things so seriously? Actually, children have a tremendous sense of humor. A parent who is willing to be a little silly encourages it to grow. Make up silly sentences that turn something into something else. For example, "What if mice were giraffes, wouldn't they look funny with long necks eating leaves from the top of tall trees? "What if we lived in a tree like a squirrel?" Then let your child make one up. The possibilities are endless. This is a great car game; don't be surprised if your child asks to play it daily.

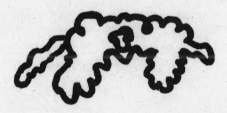

Joke Books

There are many joke and riddle books, such as school age jokes, knock-knock jokes, jokes about dinosaurs, and numerous joke websites. Buy a book or check out a website to find a riddle or joke to tell. Help your children to learn the ones they like so they can tell them to their friends, grandparents and teachers. Once exposed to jokes and riddles, your child may start to make up her own. Laugh at all the jokes your child makes up no matter how silly. Remember, they are just learning, and your smile and laughter will encourage them to keep trying.

Read Funny Stories and Poems

Being exposed to funny stories broadens a child's imagination. The following is a list of funny books that you might look for at the library:

For two- to five-year-olds:

"The Little Boy Laughed" by Lucy Cousins

"Cloudy With a Chance of Meatballs" by Judi Barrett

"Thomas' Snowsuit" by Robert Munsch

For five- to ten-year-olds:

"Ready...Set...Read-and Laugh: A Funny Treasury for Beginning Readers" by Cole and Calmenson

"Laughing Out Loud" by Jack Prelutsky

For ten- to twelve-year-olds:

"Alpha Beta Chowder" by Jeanne and William Steig (poetry)

"The Great All-Time Excuse Book" by Maureen Kushner (this is my daughter's favorite, and a great one for pre-teens because it gives them some power in a funny way. Here's her favorite excuse: "Why don't you answer my question?" "I'm waiting for the multiple choice.")

If you have found any favorite books, write to us at Sourcebooks so we can add to the list!

Change the Story

A fun way to add humor to that story you have read for the tenth time is to change it without telling your child. Make it silly, change the characters' parts, put it in another location, have them say a word backwards, have the characters say funny things to your child like, "if you want to know what happens next stand on your head." It's also fun to tell a story simply by looking at the pictures and not reading the words. That way you can make it as silly as you want to. Your child will like to tell you stories too, so encourage the budding storyteller.

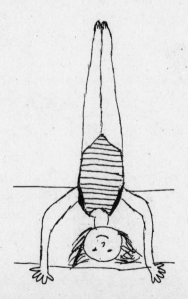

Funniest Home Videos

Here's your chance to be movie stars. If you don't have a video camera, borrow one from a friend for the night. Think about things that might look funny on camera, or simply try to capture people doing things naturally that are funny. Children are very good at coming up with ideas, so let them be the directors. Once you have taped the funny acts, sit in front of the TV and watch them. It won't matter whether they are funny or not; the kids will laugh watching themselves trying to be funny.

Can You Top This? Contest

Funny things happen all the time in families: someone puts on the wrong pair of underwear, the kids are having a backwards running race and someone runs into the lake, mom answers the phone and talks for five minutes before realizing it was the school principal and not her best friend, someone says the wrong word in a sentence, etc. It doesn't always feel good when you are the person who does the funny thing; sometimes, it is embarrassing and feels like people are laughing at you. Often the best thing a child can learn to do in an embarrassing situation is laugh. Parents can help children develop a sense of humor by

sharing the funny, embarrassing things that happen to them on a daily basis. Have an after dinner "Can You Top This" contest. The only rule is that the funny situation has to happen naturally, it can't be created just for the contest. Each person share anything funny they saw or did that day and the family votes on the funniest.

Making Fun of Someone

Children need to learn that making jokes about other people hurts all people. It is never funny when a child calls another child fat, and all the children laugh. The only way to stop this from happening is to do the following when you hear it. Take the time to ask your child what they think is funny about what they said? Then have them close their eyes and pretend they were the person the joke was about. How would they feel? Let them tell you out loud how they would feel. It may take a few times to sink in, but if each time they have to think what another person might feel, they will learn compassion and that humor should not be mean.

Make Me Laugh Game

It's fun to try to make someone else laugh. The following games can be played with everyone sitting in a circle, or two people sitting across from each other:

- Pass the laugh: the first person says "Ha" with a straight face, the next person says "Ha, Ha" with a straight face. You keep adding Ha's until someone laughs. That person is out of the game.
- Pass the face: in this game you take turns making funny faces until someone laughs.
- Have a staring contest. You stare at each other with no expression until someone starts to laugh.

Silly Sentence Play

If your family is dramatic, here's a fun one for you. First, on index cards, write down twenty sentences like the following:

> Look, a cat climbed through the window!
> I have to go to the toilet.
> Can you believe what Allen did?
> That was the day of the earthquake.

Next, decide on a scene to act out, like going to the zoo, riding horses, taking a test at school, or attending a birthday party. Place all the sentence cards face down on the floor where you will be acting out the scene. Begin acting out the play, and whenever someone feels like it, they can pick up a card and read what it says. The sentences always sound funny because they are completely off the subject! Make up more sentences and keep playing. This might be a fun activity to video tape.

Hands That Make You Laugh

You need two people for this activity. One person stands or sits directly in front of another with their hands behind their back. Try not to let the front person's arms show. The person in back extends their arms around the front person and does all the hand movements. The person in front makes faces and talks. The audience can shout out scenes for the pair to act out that would involve many hand movements: eating in the school cafeteria, brushing teeth and washing face, father shaving, putting a model together, painting a picture, etc. Let everyone in the family have a chance to make the family laugh.

Traditions

Traditions are the things we do in family, year after year, that create lasting memories to be carried on into the life of the next generation. When a family shares traditions they build a special bond of shared experience. The traditions we choose determine our family's unique way of experiencing life together. They become a sort of map that illustrates the journey the family has been on.

"Remembering the past gives power to the present."
—Faye Myenne Ng

Start a Family Tradition

A family tradition is a customary way of doing something which is handed down over time. It is something everyone in the family enjoys doing over and over, something ordinary made very special. Traditions create closer families. Think of the things you do together as a family that you might want to pass down to future generations. Remember, traditions don't have to be old, they can be created today. Here are a few ideas:

Sharing donuts on Sunday morning
A monthly hike on the full moon
Going to a certain school
Afternoon tea
Discussions after dinner

The possibilities are endless. Think of one tradition that your family wants to begin today, and begin it.

Good Wishes

"Find a penny, pick it up, all day long you'll have good luck!" Through the ages, the penny has come to symbolize good luck. Wishing on a penny and giving it to a family member shows you care. Fill a glass container with pennies; this will be your wishing bank. Start the tradition off on a special occasion like a birthday, graduation, first or last day of school, special achievement or award, new job, engagement, or wedding. When it's time to make penny wishes, each well-wisher takes a penny from the wishing bank and gives it as they tell their wish. It's also possible for penny wishes to be given individually, to someone who might be sick, downhearted, scared, or in need of encouragement. If family members live far away, why not send them a penny wish in the mail?

It's Immaterial

When your next gift-giving holiday arrives, consider starting the tradition of giving non-material gifts. As a family, talk about the non-material gifts you received during the past year: a friend's laughter, a helping hand, special words of encouragement, someone's appearance at a performance or event, a tender touch, a shoulder to cry on, practical advice, being listened to, a happy experience, or an understanding friend. Then each of you privately choose a non-material gift to give each person you love. Write or draw what it is, put it in an envelope, and give it with joy!

Celebrate the Firsts

An individual life has many events that are considered "firsts." Decide on traditional ways of celebrating these firsts that will be passed down to each child in the family; treat the child to a special event of their choice, have a family party, present them with a piece of jewelry. During this time, listen carefully as the child talks about her life event that's being recognized. Share your experiences of the same 'first' in your life. Let children know how proud you are of who they are.

Birthday Traditions

Birthday traditions are fun to create. For the next family member's birthday, why not try one of the following?

Birthday Book—Using an oversized blank book or scrapbook, start to create a family birthday book. From now on, every person's birthday gets captured in words, photos, impressions, stories, drawings, or poetry, contributed by all family members. Even the youngest can make a hand or foot print on the page. As years pass, it's fun to go back and read about each person's special day.

Sheet of Notes—Buy a large white sheet to be used as a tablecloth at a birthday party. Make sure to put a piece of plastic underneath it. Have permanent fabric markers around the table so people can write the birthday person a note. Make sure to date the note because the sheet will be used each year on that person's birthday. You may want to wait until after dinner to put the sheet on the table so that it isn't full of food stains!

Your Cultural Traditions

If you are having a hard time coming up with new family traditions that excite the group, why not look to the past. What is your cultural heritage? Visit the library together to get information about your cultural traditions or research on the internet a website that offers cultural recipes and customs. This could be a family project. Look specifically for pictures and descriptions of customs. When information is gathered, set a date to talk about it; then, plan a day to experience a cultural tradition. If everyone likes it, keep it; if not, try another one.

Personal Song

Take the time to make up a song about each member of your family. The song should be written to a tune that everyone knows, such as that person's favorite childhood lullaby. The words might be the person's name sung repeatedly, a loving wish repeated (I'll always love you; You're always in my thoughts; My heart sings for you), acknowledgment of a special trait (your sunny disposition, generous spirit, gentle touch, kind way of speaking), or a favorite activity (you're the best swimmer, the hardest worker, most talented artist). Write down the words so that the song can be sung repeatedly throughout the person's life.

Thanks for the Year

Pick a day for everyone in the family to say what they are thankful for from the past year; Thanksgiving, New Years Day, or Valentines day all work well. All you do is describe the things that happened in your life for which you are grateful. Don't forget all the simple things, like having a place to live, food, a peaceful country, and a family that cares. Each person gets a chance to talk, and everyone needs to listen quietly without comment.

Traditional Clean-Up

Anybody can start something. It could even become a tradition if it gets repeated enough times. Your family could originate an annual community clean-up day, picking up trash from roadways, parks, riverbeds, or other public areas. Don't be discouraged, this will be easier than you think. Decide on a date and a location to clean up. Pick the time and spot that everyone will meet. Have all the family help make a flyer. Include this information: the date, time, and place of the clean up, what you are doing, suggestions that people bring bags for the trash, whether they should bring drinks and snacks, and your name and phone number in case they have questions. Let the kids help distribute the flyer to friends, neighbors, schools, and local businesses. All you have to do is show up and enjoy the community feel of working together. If you're doing something you believe in, you'll be happy no matter how few or how many others show up. Every tradition starts somewhere.

What Is Ritual?

Ritual brings meaning to otherwise ordinary things. It is something the family does to make an ordinary task special, drawing everyone closer because of the shared meaning. Get everyone together and see if anyone has any ideas of ways to make ordinary things, like mealtimes, bedtime, departures, arrivals, rainy days, cleaning the house, celebrations, etc., more special through ritual. Here are some ideas: light a candle before dinner and say something; hug each other before bed; go out in the rain together the first rainy day of the season; cut the first flower of spring seen in your yard, and each person take a petal with them to school or work; say sweet dreams each night before bed to each person. The possibilities are endless. The result will be that your family shares special moments. Shared memories build security and a sense of belonging.

Share Something

Create a sharing ritual. If there is ever something that a family member wants to share with the family, they could put it in the middle of the dinner table. That way everyone will know that during or after dinner, something will be shared. It might be a report card, work report, party invitation, art piece, recital announcement, or a picture of the animal you want to get. If it's an experience to be shared, the person simply writes their name on a small piece of paper and places it in the middle of the table. If the family doesn't eat dinner together, plan time in the evening for everyone to come to the table if there is an object on the table that needs to be shared.

Do you like my new Dress?

Candle

Lighting a candle doesn't ordinarily have special meaning. It can though, if you connect the lighting with a special shared thought. With the family together, light a candle for a special purpose that everyone agrees on. Possible purposes for lighting might be to give support to someone, encouraging a particular success, mourning a loss, celebrating a victory, expressing thanks, affirming decisions and commitments, or asking for help. Sharing the thought and the purpose can create its own tradition.

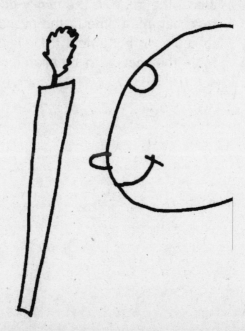

Farewell

Even when a family member goes away for a while on a trip, to camp, off for schooling or training, a hospitalization, a job or service, we remain connected to them through our thoughts and shared life experiences. Make a few small pouches out of fabric big enough to hold a few trinkets. Sew Velcro on the top to close it, or lace a string around the top like a drawstring. Make it a family ritual that when anyone leaves for a while, they take with them some small thing from each person contained in the pouch. It could be a feather, leaf, stone, small clay figure, a piece of candy, anything that would remind the person of that family member.

About the Author

Dedicated mother of four, prolific author, founder of community youth and mentoring programs and nationally recognized speaker on successful parenting, Sheila Ellison is the consummate mother of the millennium. Her advice has been helping more than 400,000 parents creatively feed, play with and raise their children. Ellison created and coauthored the 365 series of parenting books, including *365 Days of Creative Play* and *365 Foods Kids Love to Eat*.

Barbara Ann Barnett is a licensed clinical psychologist in private practice in the San Francisco Bay area, and is the mother of an adult son. It is her great hope that this book will contribute to the psychological health of families around the world, with special benefits to the children.

Notes

_____

_____

_____

_____

_____

_____

_____

_____

_____

_____

_____

_____

Notes

Notes

Notes

Notes

_____

_____

_____

_____

_____

_____

_____

_____

_____

_____

_____

_____

Notes

Notes

Notes

Notes

Notes

_____

_____

_____

_____

_____

_____

_____

_____

_____

_____

_____

_____

Notes

_____

_____

_____

_____

_____

_____

_____

_____

_____

_____

_____

_____

Notes

Notes

Notes

Notes

_____

_____

_____

_____

_____

_____

_____

_____

_____

_____

_____

_____